GEORGE ABBOT
THE UNWANTED ARCHBISHOP

BY THE SAME AUTHOR:

Lancelot Andrewes, 1555-1626
How the Church of England Works
The Bond of Church and State

GEORGE ABBOT
From a portrait in the National Portrait Gallery

GEORGE ABBOT
THE
UNWANTED ARCHBISHOP
1562–1633

by

PAUL A. WELSBY

LONDON
S · P · C · K
1962

First published in 1962
by S.P.C.K.
Holy Trinity Church
Marylebone Road
London N.W.1
Made and printed in Great Britain by
William Clowes and Sons, Limited, London and Beccles

TO

THE BISHOP AND CLERGY OF

THE DIOCESE OF

ST EDMUNDSBURY AND IPSWICH

Acknowledgements

Thanks are due to the following for permission to quote from copyright sources:

George Allen & Unwin Ltd: Thomas Fuller, *The Worthies of England*, ed. J. Freeman.

The American Philosophical Society and Professor Norman E. McClure: *The Letters of John Chamberlain*.

Faber & Faber Ltd and Harcourt, Brace & World, Inc.; T. S. Eliot. "East Coker", in *Four Quartets*.

Faber & Faber Ltd: William McElwee, *The Murder of Sir Thomas Overbury*.

The Editor of *The Listener* and Canon Charles Smyth: a broadcast, "Scholarship in the Service of Religion", 30 October 1947

Longmans, Green & Co. Ltd: *John Gerard, the Autobiography of an Elizabethan*, tr. P. Caraman; Farrar, Straus & Cudahy, Inc.: the American edition of this book, entitled *The Autobiography of a Hunted Priest*.

Macmillan & Co. Ltd: H. R. Trevor-Roper, *Archbishop Laud*.

Martin Secker & Warburg Ltd: Aubrey, *Brief Lives*, ed. O. L. Dick.

Grateful acknowledgement is made to the following for permission to use the above illustrations: The Trustees of the National Portrait Gallery; The Victoria County History, University of London; The Lambeth Palace Library; The Earl of Verulam, F.R.G.S., J.P.; and The Master and Governors of Trinity Hospital, Guildford.

Contents

Illustrations

Preface

WHEN I WAS writing the biography of that shadowy and overpraised seventeenth-century divine, Lancelot Andrewes, I was ever conscious that perpetually lurking in the background was George Abbot, the far from shadowy Archbishop of Canterbury. There has been no full-scale biography of Abbot, and the only sketches of his career and character are those in the *Biographia Britannica* and the *Dictionary of National Biography*, together with allusions in the works of such authors as Thomas Fuller, Peter Heylyn, David Lloyd, and the Earl of Clarendon. Yet George Abbot was Primate of All England for no less than twenty-two years during a period of great importance in the history of the Church of England. In view of these facts it seemed appropriate that a study of Archbishop Abbot should be attempted.

My thanks are due to a number of people who have been kind enough to answer my requests for information. They include Sir David L. Keir, Master of Balliol College, Oxford, Mr R. B. McCallum, Master of Pembroke College, Oxford, Mr A. D. M. Cox, Senior Tutor of University College, Oxford, the late Dr Norman Sykes, Mr William Urry, Keeper of MSS., Canterbury Cathedral, Mr Michael B. S. Exham, Lichfield Diocesan Registrar, Dr E. M. Dance, Guildford Borough Archivist, and Major J. Mostyn, Master of Trinity Hospital, Guildford. To this list I would add the staff and officials of the British Museum Reading Room and MSS. Room, the Cambridge University Library, the London Guildhall Library, the Lambeth Palace Library, and the Ipswich Borough Library. Mr R. A. Christophers of Bramley, Guildford, kindly allowed me to make use of the bibliographical thesis on printed works by and about Abbot, which he wrote for the Diploma in Librarianship of London University, and gave me much useful information of a bibliographical nature.

Finally, I would once again acknowledge my debt to my wife, who in various ways has contributed greatly towards the smooth progress of my work.

Copdock,   PAUL A. WELSBY
Ipswich.
May, 1962.

Abbreviations

NOTE:

Spelling and punctuation of contemporary sources have been
modernized.

I

"Bred up a Scholar"

Studies serve for delight, for ornament, and for ability. Their chief use for delight, is in privateness and retiring; for ornament, is in discourse; and for ability, is in the judgement of business.

FRANCIS BACON, *Essay: Of Studies*

In most of our colleges there are also great numbers of students, of which many are found by the revenues of the houses and other by the purveyances and help of their rich friends.

WILLIAM HARRISON, *Description of England*

TWENTY-TWO YEARS is a long period in the history of a Church that is being beset by forces which tend towards disruption. If for those twenty-two years it lacks effective leadership, the consequences may well be grave. For that number of years, at the beginning of the seventeenth century, George Abbot reigned at Lambeth as Primate of All England. Between the appointment of Thomas Cranmer in 1533 and the imprisonment of William Laud in 1634, a period of about a hundred years, there were eight Archbishops of Canterbury, and Abbot held the See longer than any of the others except Cranmer. It is a sad fact that in Abbot's case length of days was unmatched by any corresponding wealth of achievement, in spite of his personal goodness, moral integrity, and steadfastness of purpose.

Of the eight Archbishops between the Reformation and the Revolution, one (Reginald Pole) was an anachronism and two (Edmund Grindal and George Abbot) were a mistake. The rest, through force of character, breadth of vision, or administrative ability, led the Church of England along the paths of greatness. Thomas Cranmer had been Henry VIII's chief instrument for the overthrowing of the Papal Supremacy and had been one of the most influential counsellors of Edward VI. He was largely responsible for the influence in England of the continental Reformers,

I

with all its attendant consequences, although his greatest legacy, bearing the marks of his masterly English style and his superb liturgical craftsmanship, was the Book of Common Prayer. Cardinal Reginald Pole, who succeeded him and aided the Roman reaction under Mary Tudor, although he represented a deviation in the course of the evolution of the Church of England, was a man of parts and was animated by an intense singleness of purpose.

Matthew Parker cannot be regarded as a forceful Primate, but he contributed a sense of stability to the Church after the Marian upheaval, and with wisdom and tolerance faced a considerable Puritan opposition. He took part in the issue of the Thirty-nine Articles of Religion and the Bishops' Bible. It was in the realm of scholarship, however, that he made his supreme contribution, and the Church of England is indebted to him for "the criterion of sound learning, and in particular for the appeal to history and the material for that appeal. . . . The victory of Anglicanism was won by Archbishop Whitgift in the realm of ecclesiastical policy, and by Richard Hooker in the realm of controversial divinity: but what had made the victory possible was the patient, modest, resolute statesmanship of Archbishop Parker. In that age of explosive personalities, his mild and moderating temper was a considerable asset to both Church and Commonwealth."[1]

Under Archbishop Grindal a noticeable deterioration set in. Grindal was pious and upright, but of strong Puritan sympathies and lax in enforcing discipline. Puritanism increased, and Grindal refused to obey the Queen's command to suppress the Puritan prophesyings. As a consequence he was sequestered from his jurisdiction, and for five years, "just when the Church needed not secular control but strong spiritual leadership against both the Romanists and non-conformists, its authority was largely undermined and weakened".[2] Grindal was succeeded in 1583 by a man whose life was dedicated to the service of the Church—"a man born for the benefit of his country and the good of his Church".[3] Patient and persistent, John Whitgift laboured with shining

---

[1] Charles Smyth, "Scholarship in the Service of Religion", in *The Listener*, 30 Oct. 1947, pp. 767 f.

[2] V. J. K. Brook, *Whitgift and the English Church* (1957), p. 76.

[3] J. Strype, quoted V. J. K. Brook, op. cit., p. 183.

integrity to infuse spiritual vitality into the Church of England. Possessed of a strong personality, with a clear understanding of his goal, he repressed Puritanism and resisted Papal influence, and worked untiringly to raise the intellectual, spiritual, and pastoral status of the clergy. His policy was continued with greater relentlessness by Richard Bancroft, an outstanding administrator, who did much to enforce Church Law and to improve the lot of the clergy.[1]

Such were Abbot's predecessors. His successor was the controversial and unsympathetic William Laud, who made a great and tragic impact upon the Church. His enforcement of uniformity, which earned him such odium, was in obedience to his vision of what he believed a national Catholic Church should be. His methods were violent and his manner autocratic, and this made his ecclesiastical policy one of the causes of the subsequent national upheaval which well-nigh destroyed the Church. As the clouds cleared, however, it was seen that he too had left a legacy which was to endure, for "Laud stood for the dual principle of maintaining 'a uniformity in the external worship of God according to the doctrine and discipline of the Church' while allowing, on that basis, a generous freedom of theological speculation".[2]

George Abbot possessed neither the statesmanship and capacity of Cranmer, the scholarship and wisdom of Parker, nor the administrative ability and vision of Whitgift, Bancroft, and Laud. Of the eight Archbishops of the period, Abbot resembles most closely Edmund Grindal, the least effective of them all. Like Grindal he was a man of pious and upright character; like Grindal he was of Puritan sympathies and lacked zeal for discipline; like Grindal he had the moral courage to withstand the royal will and, as in the case of Grindal, the result was sequestration. The main difference—and it is the crucial one—was that whereas the Church of England had to endure Edmund Grindal for seven years, George Abbot was Archbishop for twenty-two.

George Abbot was born at Guildford on Thursday 29 October 1562, the second son of Maurice Abbot, who had married Alice March (or Marsh). Maurice Abbot was a clothworker who

---

[1] For a fuller estimate of Bancroft's achievements, see below, pp. 37f.
[2] Charles Smyth, art. cit.

inhabited a cottage near the bridge over the River Wey in the parish of St Nicholas.[1] He and his wife were staunch Protestants and had suffered persecution at the hands of Dr John Story during the reign of Queen Mary.[2] They had six sons, three of whom rose to eminence. The eldest, Robert, became Bishop of Salisbury; the second, George, became Archbishop of Canterbury; and the youngest, Maurice, became a wealthy City merchant, served as Lord Mayor of London, and was the first person to receive a knighthood from Charles I. The parents died within ten days of each other in 1606, both of them being over eighty.

John Aubrey recorded the curious anecdote that Alice Abbot, shortly before the birth of her son George, "did long for a Jack or Pike, and she dreamt that if she should Eat a Jack, her Son in her Belly should be a *great Man*. Upon this she was indefatigable to satisfy her Longing, as well as her Dream. . . . Next Morning, going with her Pail to the River-side . . . to take up some Water, a good Jack accidentally came into her Pail. She took up the much desired Banquet, dress'd it, and devour'd it almost all her self, or very near."[3] Aubrey declared that this anecdote "is generally received for a truth", and maintained that it had certain beneficial material consequences for the family. "The odd Affair made no small Noise in the Neighbourhood, and the Curiosity of it made several People of Quality offer themselves to be Sponsors at the Baptismal Font . . . and three were chosen, who maintained him at School, and University afterwards, his father not being able." Now Aubrey was the first person to publish this. He did so in 1694, and it is curious that earlier writers, such as Thomas Fuller and David Lloyd, do not appear to know of it. If it had been current in their day, it would surely have been recorded by them, for both Fuller and Lloyd had a propensity for noting the marvellous, and in any case its consequences were supposed to have influenced the future career of Abbot. It is probable that, like all legends, it had some basis in fact and stems from the natural question of how the son of a family which was not over-blessed with wealth was able to receive his education at Oxford. That Abbot did receive help

---

[1] The cottage later became "The Three Mariners Inn" and remained standing until 1864—J. Aubrey, *Brief Lives* (ed. O. L. Dick, 1949), p. 3.

[2] Thomas Fuller, *Abel Redivivus* (1651), p. 540.

[3] J. Aubrey, *Brief Lives* (ed. O. L. Dick, 1949), p. 3.

from local citizens and friends finds some support in the fact that in his later years Abbot showed a real concern for his birthplace and was one of its most munificent benefactors. It was as though he felt that he owed a debt to Guildford.

George Abbot was baptized in St Nicholas's Church on 30 October the day after his birth. He received his early education at the Free Grammar School at Guildford, which is believed to have been founded in or before 1507 by Robert Beckingham, a London grocer, and which received a Royal Charter and endowments from King Edward VI. The headmaster during Abbot's time at the school was Francis Taylor,[1] but there is no evidence of Abbot's progress or manner of life during his schooldays.

In September 1579, at the age of sixteen, he entered Balliol College, Oxford, as a scholar, but does not appear to have matriculated until 1581.[2] The subjects taught at Oxford were virtually the same as those prescribed in the time of Edward VI, and consisted of theology, law, philosophy, medicine, mathematics, dialectic, rhetoric, Greek, and Hebrew. A scholar would be expected to attend certain specified lectures and to participate in academic exercises, the chief of which were disputations. According to the regulations scholars were supposed to reside for sixteen terms (four years) before they could secure the B.A. degree, but dispensations commonly dispensed with one or more terms of residence. Thus Abbot received his degree in 1582, three years after his entry into college.[3] He was ordained and in 1583 was elected a probationary Fellow of his college.[4] He remained Fellow for fourteen years and during that time held various college offices.[5] He became Master of Arts in November 1585,[6] and in March 1597 he proceeded Doctor of Divinity,[7] on the occasion of which he read in the theological school a dissertation entitled *Questiones sex totidem praelectionibus in Schola*

---

[1] Anthony à Wood, *Athenae Oxonienses* (ed. J. Bliss, 1813–20), II, cols. 224, 561.

[2] *Balliol College Annual Lists,* compiled by Andrew Clark in 1909; J. Foster, *Alumni Oxonienses* (1887–9), I, p. 1.

[3] Ibid.

[4] Balliol College Register, 1514–1682; *Balliol College Annual Lists.*

[5] Junior Dean, 1587 and 1589; Junior Bursar, 1588 and 1590; Senior Dean, 1592, 1595, and 1596; Notary, 1597—*Balliol College Annual Lists.*

[6] Ibid.   [7] Ibid.

Theologica Oxoniae, pro forma habitis, discussae et disceptatae anno 1597, in quibus è sacra Scriptura et Patribus, quid statuendum sit definitur.[1] This work reveals that Abbot was already a forthright Puritan. This is what one would expect, for in his childhood he had been brought up in a family which had a staunch affection for the reformed faith and had suffered for it under Queen Mary, and when he arrived at Oxford he would find little there to turn him from his principles and much to confirm him in them. Although Cambridge University was the chief academic centre for the Puritan movement, Oxford also was in a real sense a Puritan stronghold, although it had no such conspicuous leader as Cambridge had in Thomas Cartwright. Many of the college tutors were steeped in Calvinism. Laurence Humphrey, President of Magdalen, and Thomas Sampson, Dean of Christ Church, were prominent Puritans, while the Chancellor of the University, the Earl of Leicester, himself favoured the Puritan party. In one respect Oxford outshone Cambridge and that was in the prominent part she played in the education of the secular leaders of the Puritan cause in Parliament. Three of the five members whom Charles I attempted to arrest in 1641 were Oxford men—Hampden, Pym, and Strode—while other prominent leaders, such as Lord Saye and Sele, Sir Henry Vane (junior), John Selden, and Oliver St John, were Oxonians.

It may be said that while there was little of the fanaticism, the excitement, and the rebelliousness which characterized the Puritan ferment at Cambridge, there was at Oxford a more restrained but none the less tenacious and widespread Puritan movement, which increased in importance as the years passed. Such an atmosphere was acceptable to Abbot, with his family background. The austere doctrine of predestination was congenial to his gloomy and morose temperament, and he became " stiffly principled" in Puritan doctrine. It was not so much that he absorbed the Puritan atmosphere of Oxford as that he contributed to it, and during his fourteen years residence Balliol, which during the reign of Queen Mary had been strongly Catholic, became noted for its Puritanism. Abbot's influence became even more apparent when he was Master of University College and

[1] Published 1598.

6

entered into controversy with William Laud. Yet he was never an extreme left-wing Puritan, for he possessed a horror of disorder and consequently detested the Separatists and those whose Puritanism led them into a contempt for authority and order. He was indeed a Calvinist in doctrine, but he did not countenance free forms of worship nor the presbyterian or congregational forms of Church government. Above all he was a staunch upholder of episcopacy, although he saw it not as a divinely appointed separate order of ministry but as a most convenient and ancient form of ecclesiastical superintendence. From these convictions, arrived at or confirmed by his experience at Oxford, he never wavered, and from them stemmed in due course some of his weaknesses when he became Archbishop of Canterbury.

George Abbot won a reputation as an efficient lecturer and as a powerful preacher. As a Fellow of his college he would not only have had the task of formal lecturing but he would also have been engaged in tutorial instruction, and "the work of the college tutors rather than the readings of the college lecturers was probably in the sixteenth century the most important influence on a scholar's education".[1] The reason for this was that it was through the tutorial that scholars received an education more liberal, broader, and more enriching than that provided by the statutory lectures and disputations: for whereas the fields of study covered by the latter were governed by strict regulation, college tutors were not thus restricted and could therefore instruct their pupils in many of the liberal arts, such as history, geography, and modern languages. M. H. Curtis has pointed out[2] that there was in Oxford at the end of the sixteenth century a group of younger men who had interests in scientific and kindred subjects, such as mathematics, astronomy, cosmography, and geography, and whose work both within and outside the University helped to advance knowledge about these subjects in an age when they were not taken seriously by the University itself. It would appear that Abbot was one of the lesser lights of this group. In 1599 he published a work on geography, entitled *A Brief Description of the*

---

[1] M. H. Curtis, *Oxford and Cambridge in Transition, 1558–1642* (1959), p. 107.
[2] Ibid., pp. 120, 236.

7

Whole World. Wherein is particularly described all the Monarchies, Empires, and Kingdoms of the Same. This book had originally been compiled for the use of his pupils[1] and it later ran through no less than seven or eight editions, which testifies to the popularity of such works. E. G. R. Taylor has described it as an "arid compilation", which "is for the most part a mere catalogue of place-names, forerunner of the dreary geographies which held the field in English schools right down to the twentieth century".[2] This is an unfair judgement, for although the work is not wildly exciting by modern standards, Abbot was pioneering in a new field. Neither is it a true statement of fact to describe it as "a mere catalogue of place-names", for Abbot describes both geographical features and the forms and revenues of ecclesiastical and civil governments. For example, when he wrote about Italy he included a comment on the Papacy which would hardly appear in "a mere catalogue of place-names". "The Bishops of Rome", he wrote, "do pretend that *Constantine* the great, did bestow upon them the City of Rome, together with divers other Cities and Towns near adjoining. . . . But *Laurentius Valla* in his set Treatise of this argument, hath displayed the falsehood of that pretence: and in truth, the greatness of the *Popes* has risen first by *Phocas* who . . . did . . . suffer the Bishop of Rome to be proclaimed *Universal Bishop* . . . And afterwards *King Pepin of France*, and *Charles* the great his son getting (by means of the said Bishop) the kingdom of France, and the one of them to the Empire, did bestow good possessions upon the Papacy."[3] There is a curious appendix to the work, giving a list of the Universities in the world, together with the latitude and longitude of each.[4] It may well be that it

[1] Anthony à Wood, *Athenae Oxonienses* (ed. J. Bliss, 1813-20), II, pp. 361 f; *D.N.B.*, "Abbot, George".

[2] E. G. R. Taylor, *Late Tudor and Early Stuart Geography, 1583-1650* (1934), p. 37.

[3] *A Brief Description of the Whole World* (1605 ed.). Pages unnumbered.

[4] In 1613 Samuel Purchas published *Purchas his Pilgrimage* and dedicated the work to George Abbot. Whether this was a tribute to Abbot's reputation as a geographer or was due to less worthy motives is not known, but Purchas had his immediate reward by being made chaplain to the Archbishop— E. G. R. Taylor, *Late Tudor and Early Stuart Geography, 1583-1650* (1934), p. 55. H. Savage, in *Balliofergus, or a Commentary upon the Foundation, Founders and Affairs of Balliol College,* claimed that Peter Heylyn took Abbot's *Brief Description* as a model for his *Microcosmus* (1621).

was this early interest in places beyond the sea, together with his brother Maurice's concern with their commercial potentialities, that led Abbot to associate himself in later life with the adventurers to Virginia, in which he held seventy-five shares.[1]

Very few of Abbot's sermons have survived, but the most extensive collection consists of a long series of lecture-sermons on the book of Jonah[2] which he gave at the University between 1594 and 1599. The first reaction to these sermons is one of amazement that anyone should find so much to say about one of the shortest books in the Old Testament. It is even more startling that a preacher should have sufficient perseverance to concentrate on one book for such a long period. The book of Jonah contains four short chapters, comprising a total of forty-eight verses. From this material Abbot contrives to produce thirty sermons, covering 638 quarto pages.[3] He began the series in 1594 and completed it five years later. The main reason why it took him so long was because, in accordance with custom, he took his turn with other preachers. He himself was aware that he was spending an unconscionable time over the undertaking, for he prefaced the twenty-fourth sermon with an apology because "before that I can come to this fourth chapter [of Jonah], the fourth year has now expired". He excused himself on the grounds that he would have got on more speedily "if either this place had called him oftener to it, or other occasions had not elsewhere diverted him".[4] The sermons were preached in St Mary's, Oxford, on Thursday mornings, sometimes before daylight, and—according to the preacher—they were well attended not only by young people but also by "the elder and stronger sort".

Abbot did not question the historicity of Jonah, and he went into considerable details of speculation about his parentage. He also accepted the view that Jonah wrote his story himself.[5] The identity of the "great fish" is discussed at some length, with the assistance of quotations from Olaus Magnus, Gulielmus,

---

[1] *The Records of the Virginia Company of London* (ed. S. M. Kingsbury, 1906), III, pp. 80–90.

[2] *Exposition on the Prophet Jonah, in certain Sermons preached at St Mary's Church in Oxford* (1600). Quotations are from the 1865 edition.

[3] In the 1600 edition.

[4] I, p. 201.   [5] I, p. 26.

Rondeletius, Pliny, Dion, Gesner, St Augustine, and St Jerome.[1]
Like most commentators on Jonah, he saw in the event of Jonah
and the great fish a type of Christ's Resurrection. "Jonah was in
the fish's belly, so was Christ in the grave; Jonah came forth
thence, so did Christ rise again; his rising doth bring our
rising—his resurrection ours, because he was the first fruits of
all those that do sleep."[2]

The sermons took the form of an expository commentary on
each verse, or part-verse, of the book. The text is analysed and
explained and is then used as a peg upon which to hang dogmatic
and hortatory teaching, each sermon leading into and ending
with a doxology. The style is vigorous and swiftly moving, such
as to retain the interest of the hearers. There is an absence of any
of the word-play, so characteristic of the medieval tradition of
sermon making, which had been perpetuated by Abbot's contemporary, Lancelot Andrewes.[3] The sermons reveal the preacher's
wide knowledge of the Eastern and Western Fathers and of the
Latin and Greek classical writers, and his adroitness in linking
together passages of the Scriptures to illustrate and further his
theme. For example, in discussing God's omnipresence he brings
together with great effect Jonah 1.3, Ps. 139, Gen. 3.8, and
Rev. 6.15.[4] Again, in dealing with the casting of lots in Jonah 1.7,
he quotes or refers to Josh. 7.18, 1 Sam. 14.42, Acts 1.26, Prov.
16.32 and 18.18, Esther, Josh. 16.1, Homer, St Augustine, Josephus,
and Tacitus.[5] Abbot had the gift of composing a vivid phrase. He
described Jonah as "the testiest man who ever lived, he did fret
and scold with God",[6] and he spoke of thoughts "tumbling at
this time in the working head of Jonah".[7] In order to drive home
his point he made telling use of illustrations.

> In a wreck at sea, a board oftentimes doth save a man from
> drowning by his lying fast thereupon; but if he be beaten by
> the violence of the sea from this first plank, and be now floating
> in the water, if a second by some accident be afforded him, and
> he can keep him fast thereto, it setteth him free from all danger.

[1] I, pp. 198 ff.   [2] I, p. 217.
[3] See Paul A. Welsby, *Lancelot Andrewes, 1555–1626* (1958), pp. 194 f.
[4] I, pp. 41 f.   [5] I, pp. 86 ff.   [6] I, p. 27.
[7] I, p. 35.

It is more than apparent that we have suffered a wreck, and are driving into the sea of shame and desperation, even ready still to be drenched. The first table which relieveth us is the sacrament of baptism which . . . doth acquit us from the guilt of original sin; from the which if we be beaten off by the force of actual crimes, the second plank is repentance to be caught at, which if we hold fast and do not leave, it will bring us into the haven of blessed and quiet rest.[1]

Some of his illustrations are based on the curious scientific lore of his day.

It fares with the sinner as it doth with the crocodile, when his belly is stuffed with some prey; for then, as Pliny writes, doth he yield himself over to sleep, and leaveth his mouth open, of purpose that a little bird called trochylus may pick his teeth and make them clean; but thereupon doth the ichneumon, a kind of serpent, take occasion to creep into the belly of the crocodile; and being once in, he never ceaseth there to gnaw, till he hath eaten through his paunch. Thus doth Satan deal with us; for amidst our idleness and forgetfulness of that horror of evil which hangeth upon us, he takes possession of our souls.[2]

Again, just as cranes, when they have to fly over the sea in a storm, swallow (according to Abbot) sand and pebbles to balance themselves against the wind, so faith must be "our Ballast" as "we do cross this troublesome world of sin and great temptation".[3]

In some of the sermons there are fine passages. Two examples may be quoted.

The laws of God and men, of nature and nations, have commanded that a great regard should be borne to the life of a man, the most excellent of all God's creatures that go upon the ground—the beauty of the world, the glory of the workman, the confluence of all honour which mortality can afford—the resemblance of the Saviour while he lived upon the earth, the

[1] I, p. 260.   [2] I, p. 73.   [3] I, p. 239.

image of God himself until that time that Adam lost it—to whose absolute frame nothing wanteth but only a consideration that God has so graced him as that nothing is wanting to him . . . The Creator himself doth give it [i.e. life]; he willeth us to preserve it, that none should dare destroy it, either in ourselves or in others.[1]

Remember how that every winter the glory of the trees and all the woods is decayed; their leaves lie in the dust, their cheerful green is but blackness—the sap and life is hid in the root within the ground—all the tree doth seem as dead; but when the sun comes forward with his warming aspect, they resume their former beauty. So it is with the meadows, so it is with the flowers, and most delightful gardens: their winter is as our death, their spring like our resurrection. . . . What is our bed but a grave? what is our sleep but a death, wherein we are to ourselves as if we had never been without sense, and in darkness?—what is our hasty awaking at the sound of a bell or other noise, but as our starting up at the sound of the last trumpet, to appear before Christ's throne?[2]

Abbot's Calvinist views emerge from time to time in these sermons, as for example when he describes "the purposes of God's election in foreappointing some unto life eternal" as "a matter so immutable and unchangeable in itself, that nothing can impeach it: the flesh with her frailty, the world with his subtlety, the multitudes and millions of infernal spirits, cannot alter that decree".[3] He speaks of the perilous times he and his hearers are living in—times in which "Satan frets and rages; in which Papism is little weakened, but Atheism waxes strong, and the sins of men cry aloud; but on the other side piety waxes thin, and charity grows cold".[4] He is harsh with the critics of the church—those who "if they can declaim in the greatest assemblies against the errors of the clergy, spy a fault in their government", consider that "they are more than common men". Many of the Puritans are far more concerned with detecting in common talk "some old word which was used in Popery" than they are with deceiving their neighbours in selling and bargaining.[5]

[1] I, p. 152. [2] I, p. 215. [3] I, p. 300.
[4] I, p. 46. [5] II, p. 194.

It is well known that one of the criticisms urged against Abbot's appointment to Canterbury was the fact that he had never been a parish priest. It would appear from one passage in these sermons that he had no illusions about parish life and the troubles which beset the parochial clergy. These troubles included "the contumely of atheists and bitter hatred of papists, the invasions of upstart heretics, the wranglings of new-found schismatics . . . the civil sort with their necessity and overmuch curiosity, the ignorant with their rudeness and indisciplinable barbarism, the old with their superstitions, the young with their sports and follies". The troublesome ones would draw the clergy into quarrels and factions, and the greater the parsons' talent "the more shall be their burthen, the greater their grace be the greater shall be their crosses". Abbot emphasized that he was not listing these troubles in order to frighten men from accepting the pastoral ministry, but "to remember myself and others to prepare themselves . . . to burthens of this weight".[1] It is interesting, however, to speculate whether this realistic, if somewhat one-sided, view of the pastoral ministry frightened Abbot himself from ever accepting a parochial cure of souls.

The fact that Abbot's strong Puritan convictions did not include laxity in the order and reverence of public worship is evident in several passages in the sermons. Itinerant preaching, characteristic of the sectaries, he condemned outright, asserting that "ours is a stable profession, it is no gadding ministry: mark that".[2] As regards the clergy of the Church of England, Abbot denounced the sin of simony, the carelessness of those who "do mind that field or barn, whence corn or wood cometh to them, oftener in one month than the pulpit in a year", and the negligence of those who "can inquire for a curate where one may be had best cheap (not respecting whether he be able to teach) . . . but how the people shall be instructed, they do not regard at all".[3] Many of the clergy show little devotion in conducting public worship, but the behaviour of parishioners is far worse. "Every light occasion doth keep them away" from Divine Service. When they do go "they sit there in giddiness, neither minding God nor the minister".[4] They talk and gaze about when their souls should

[1] II, pp. 46 f. [2] I, p. 14. [3] I, p. 310.
[4] I, p. 225.

13

be receiving instruction, they meditate upon their worldly business instead upon things sacred, they delight more in the eloquence of the preacher, "or in some, what may be carped at", rather than in "how their own life may be bettered". Their prayers too are perfunctory and formal,[1] and Abbot commented that "if it be thus in public, what may be thought of those prayers which in secret are poured forth between God and ourselves?"[2]

Public worship should be an eager joy. "We should therefore resort to these sanctuaries with greediness, even as to the type of heaven; we should joy to be there, and see all others there whom we love—and a Christian man loveth every man . . . Then let us account it our happiness that we may join our prayers unto a great congregation . . . and let us press to this place as to that where bread is broken which is the very food of life".[3] Nevertheless, if Christians will *not* attend worship freely, the magistrate should compel them to go, for "it is a most blessed compulsion for a man to be driven to truth—for a woman to be forced to heaven".[4] Abbot would have carried compulsion further still, for he clearly affirms the right of rulers to enforce men to embrace the orthodox faith. In view of his later work on the High Commission it is interesting to observe his reasoning here. Faith may indeed be "the assent of the inward man" but "the means whereby men get faith are visible and external"—i.e. sermons, Sacraments, worship—and "these things Princes . . . are bound, by duty to the Highest Lord, to exercise and execute". Abbot laid great emphasis on Christ's parable of the wedding feast, with its command to "compel them to come in" (Luke 14.23), "out of which text Thomas Aquinas doth conclude and resolve that men are to be enforced unto faith". He sums up the matter thus: "We hold for an undoubted truth, that the Prince hath a power in commanding and proclaiming for God and God's religion, and all exercises of the same."[5]

There remain extant two other sermons preached by Abbot. The first was delivered in the Temple Church, London, on 6 February 1602, and our knowledge of it is due to John Manningham, who entered notes on it in his diary. Unfortunately such a

[1] I, p. 311.   [2] I, p. 225.   [3] II, pp. 263 f.
[4] Ibid.   [5] II, pp. 145 ff.

mode of transmission precludes detailed comment on the sermon, for the notes are extremely exiguous. The subject was sin and forgiveness and the treatment is marked by simplicity. Abbot still made use of telling illustrations, as the last paragraph of Manningham's notes indicates: "Sin is like a smoke, like fire, it mounteth upward, and comes even before God to accuse us; it is like a serpent in our bosom, still ready to sting us; it is the devil's daughter. A woman hath her pains in travail and delivering, but rejoiceth when she seeth a child is born; but the birth of sin is of a contrary fashion; for all the pleasure is in the bringing forth, but when it is finished and brought forth, it tormenteth us continually; they haunt us like tragical furies."[1]

Abbot was the preacher at the funeral in Westminster Abbey on 26 May 1608 of his patron, the Earl of Dorset. His sermon was afterwards printed "at the request of some honourable persons".[2] The sermon was of immense length—the opening section is dull, prosaic, and tedious—and lacked any of the brilliance and force-fulness found in the *Exposition on the Prophet Jonah,* although it resembled the latter in the use that is made of the Scriptures. It also displayed great erudition, with quotations from Herodotus, Diodorus, St Augustine, St Bernard, St Chrysostom, St Basil, St Jerome, and St Gregory. For eleven pages Abbot dwelt on the perishableness of the flesh, and then gave point to his remarks by using the "spectacle now before us" as a vivid "memorial of mortality". He proceeded, in the fashion customary upon such occasions, to eulogize the late Earl, calling to his aid the comments of the late Queen Elizabeth upon Dorset's character and career. This occupied several more pages, and then, referring to the suddenness of Dorset's death, Abbot cited a string of examples of sudden death in the Bible, the classics, and early history. He ended by reminding his congregation to "watch, for ye know not what hour your master will come".

Apart from this somewhat specialized example of his preaching, Abbot's sermons have a quality which makes them memorable, an eloquence and straightforwardness which is impressive, and a vividness which held the interest of his hearers. It is, therefore,

[1] *Diary of John Manningham* (ed. J. Bruce, 1868), p. 26.
[2] *A Sermon Preached at Westminster, May 26, 1608, at the Funeral Solemnities of the Right Hon. Thomas Earl of Dorset* (1608).

the more surprising that he was never regarded as one of the great preachers of his age and that so few of his sermons have survived. It may be that the Dorset funeral sermon is an indication that his early preaching exuberance was over and that a moroseness of character and a stiffness of personality was invading his style of preaching. Whatever the reason, it is certain that he never gained the reputation of a great preacher.

2

"A Doctor of Divinity from Oxford"

I may not suffer those with whom I have to do to disquiet the university or
college with false doctrine and schismatical opinions: I may not suffer them
openly to break and contemn those laws and statutes which they are sworn to
observe, and I to execute. . . . These be the things I have done, and these be the
things I intend to do; whereby as hitherto I have kept the place where I am in
some quiet and good order, so do I trust to continue it, both to the glory of
God, the honour of the prince, the great increase of learning, the edifying of
Christ's Church, and the commendation both of the college and the whole
university.

JOHN WHITGIFT, *Works*

I N ORDER to obtain preferment either in Church or State in
the sixteenth and seventeenth century it was necessary for a
man to have a patron of eminence and influence. John Williams
climbed the ladder of clerical preferment with the support of the
powerful Duke of Buckingham. Lancelot Andrewes had the
assistance of the Earl of Walsingham. George Abbot, because of
his staunch support of the Puritan outlook in the University of
Oxford, earned the favour of the Lord Treasurer, Thomas
Sackville, Lord Buckhurst (afterwards Earl of Dorset), who became Chancellor of the University in 1591. He first appointed
Abbot to be his chaplain, then he secured his election as Master of
University College, and finally he procured for him the Deanery
of Winchester.[1] Abbot publicly acknowledged his debt to Lord

[1] There was a story current that he obtained the deanery by simony.
James Hussey approached him—so the story went—and "after some familiar
chiding for not endeavouring advancement told him that the Deanery of
Winton was void, and to be had for £600 and that he would give him time to
think of it over night, at which time the £600 was paid, and Dr Abbot was
made Dean"—Rawlinson MSS. (Bodleian Library), B.158.

Buckhurst, for in 1601 he dedicated his *Exposition on the Prophet Jonah* to Buckhurst and wrote of his "desire to let men understand with how honourable a regard your lordship hath been pleased now for divers years to look upon me, and of your lordship's own disposition at every first occasion so to think on my preferment, as I had no reason in my conceit to look for or in any way expect".

Abbot was installed as Dean of Winchester on 6 March 1600,[1] but, owing to a gap in the Chapter Acts Book from 1600 to 1622, there is no evidence of the part he played in the life of the cathedral. Indeed, in view of the fact that Clarendon described University College as "one of the poorest colleges in Oxford",[2] it is likely that Abbot accepted the deanery in order to supplement the slender emoluments of his Mastership.[3]

In September 1597 Abbot had been unanimously elected Master of University College, although a dispensation had had to be obtained from the Chancellor because he was a member of another college.[4] He held the office until 1610, and was regarded as a strict disciplinarian. In 1608 he convened a meeting of the Fellows of the College to investigate the misdeeds of the Bursar, James Harrison. The result was that Harrison was "warned that the debts of the house owing at Michaelmas must be paid before Christmas and was threatened with expulsion if he continued his visits to the King's Head and wanderings abroad at night".[5] Abbot also waged war against the vices of the undergraduates and in one case a Freeston exhibitioner was warned that he must forfeit his exhibition unless he could give satisfaction for "*delictis*

[1] Le Neve, *Fasti Ecclesiae Anglicanae* (1854), III, p. 22. John Harris, in *History of Kent* (1719), p. 574, and J. Dart, in *History of Canterbury Cathedral* (1726), p. 173, state that Abbot was Dean of Gloucester. The mistake may have arisen from the fact that Abbot's successor at Winchester was Thomas Morton, Dean of Gloucester.

[2] Earl of Clarendon, *History of the Great Rebellion* (1717), I, p. 88. The *Valor Ecclesiasticus,* although 100 years earlier than Abbot's Mastership, shows that, in comparison with other colleges, University College was poor. It was also in great financial difficulties shortly after the Restoration, when certain Fellowships had to be sequestered owing to its impoverishment. I owe this information to A. J. M. Cox, Senior Tutor at University College.

[3] See W. Carr, *University College, Oxford* (1902), p. 95.

[4] University College Registers; W. Carr, op. cit., p. 92.

[5] W. Carr, op. cit., p. 95.

quibusdam et scandalis turpiter et contumeliose commissis".[1] On the other hand, there is evidence that some of his pupils remembered him with affection. Sir Dudley Digges, who had proved himself "a very towardly pupil", remained on terms of close intimacy with him until his death. In 1627 Abbot wrote that Digges "calleth me father, and I term his wife my daughter. His eldest son is my godson, and their children are in love accounted my grand-children."[2] Sir George Savil, another of his pupils, when he died left his son under Abbot's guardianship. There can be no doubt that the college benefited greatly under the head-ship of a Master of Abbot's character and one who had an increasing influence in University affairs. After he ceased to be Master, Abbot retained his interest in the college and in 1632 donated £100 to be spent on the purchase of books for the college library.[3]

Abbot was Vice-Chancellor of the University in 1600 and again in 1603 and 1605.[4] In this capacity he was called upon from time to time to arbitrate in theological controversies raging outside the University. One such occasion was in 1600 when the citizens of London, whose outlook was mainly Puritan, were at loggerheads with their bishop, Richard Bancroft, on the matter of the restora-tion of the crucifix in Cheapside. This crucifix, which had long stood in that place, had fallen into decay and when Bancroft ordered its restoration the citizens refused to obey and sought the advice of both Universities. Without hesitation Abbot, as Vice-Chancellor at Oxford, condemned the restoration of the crucifix,[5] on the grounds that it would encourage superstitious devotion and would thus be "a great inducement and may be a ready way to idolatry". Moreover it would encourage the Papists and would be regarded by them as "a token of the return of their faith into this land, since the monuments are not extinguished in the chief

[1] Ibid.
[2] "Archbishop Abbot his Narrative", in J. Rushworth, *Historical Collections of private passages of state . . .* (1721).
[3] University College Registers.
[4] John Le Neve, *Fasti Ecclesiae Anglicanae* (1854), III, p. 476.
[5] *Cheapside Cross Censured and Condemned by a Letter sent from the Vice-Chancellor and other Learned Men of the famous University of Oxford in Answer to a Question propounded by the Citizens of London, concerning the said Cross, in the year 1600, in which year it was beautified . . .* (1641).

street of our greatest city". Abbot's advice was that "an obelisk be set up there" in the place of the crucifix.[1] To justify his decision he quoted two incidents that had occurred at Oxford. The first was the case of a number of young men who were observed kneeling before the representation of the Crucifixion in a window in Balliol College, as a result of which the authorities had removed the window. The second was the order he had given for the burning in the market-place at Oxford of various superstitious pictures, including one in which the figure of God the Father was placed over a Crucifixion as ready to receive the soul of Jesus. The citizens of London must have rejoiced that the Vice-Chancellor was on their side, although some of them must have had their ardour dampened by his stern warning against taking the law into their own hands, for (he wrote) "I do not permit inferior men to run headlong about such matters". In the end, a compromise was reached. The crucifix was not restored, but neither was Abbot's suggestion accepted of substituting an obelisk. Instead a plain stone cross took the place of the crucifix. Nevertheless Abbot's censure had attracted attention, and the fact that his advice was not followed excited comment. "The Cross in Cheap is going up", wrote John Chamberlain to Sir Dudley Carleton, "for all your Vice-Chancellor of Oxford and some other odd divines have set down their censure against it."[2]

In 1601 the pathetic rebellion of the Earl of Essex alarmed the country, although it was speedily repressed. On 27 April Abbot wrote to Lord Buckhurst, Chancellor of the University, that "none resident in our university interested themselves" in the rebellion "at the time of its occurrence", but the previous Thursday Abraham Colfe, a graduate of Christ Church, had made a public declaration in his college hall commending Essex for his action and inveighing against the authorities who had brought about his execution. Abbot, as Vice-Chancellor, had arrested him

---

[1] "We should hardly have supposed that, instead of the erection of the Cross, the symbol of the Christian atonement, he would have advised the erection of a pyramid, the symbol of Egyptian superstition"—W. F. Hook, *Lives of the Archbishops of Canterbury* (1875), X, p. 247.

[2] Chamberlain to Carleton, 3 Feb. 1600—Chamberlain's *Letters* (ed. S. Williams, 1861), p. 102.

and committed him to safe custody until he should receive further instructions.[1]

During his second term of office, in 1603,[2] Abbot was obliged to commit 140 undergraduates to prison for disrespectfully sitting with their hats on in his presence in St Mary's Church.[3] What is of much more significance, however, is the fact that this year saw the first of the many wrangles between Abbot and William Laud, who was later to be Abbot's successor as Archbishop of Canterbury. At this period Laud was a Fellow of St John's College and a proctor of the University. He was a small, bustling, determined young man, whose theological views were anathema to Abbot, and a collision between the two was wellnigh inevitable. In the preceding year, in the course of a divinity lecture at St John's, Laud had asserted the perpetual visibility of the Church of Christ, derived from the apostles by the Church of Rome and continued in that Church until the Reformation.[4] The Puritan party in the University was scandalized because to them the Church of Christ was not visible and because Laud's words were an admission that the Papacy had fulfilled a beneficial purpose—which they would never admit. In 1603 Abbot rebuked Laud and drew up a summary of correct Puritan views on the subject. The latter was a curious work which was widely circulated in manuscript and was published anonymously in 1624.[5] Abbot's main thesis was that the visibility and true succession of the Church in pre-Reformation times was to be found not in the Church of

---

[1] Abbot and others to the Lord Treasurer, 27 April 1601—*S.P. Dom. Eliz.*, cclxxix, 67.

[2] Towards the end of 1602 the new Library that Sir Thomas Bodley had constructed had been made ready for use, and in 1608 Sir Thomas was to write that "Mr Dr Abbot", among others, had given "very special good books" to the Library—Thomas Bodley to Dr King, Dean of Christ Church and Vice-Chancellor, 30 June 1608, in *Letters of Sir Thomas Bodley to the University of Oxford, 1598–1611* (ed. G. Wheeler, 1927), p. 18.

[3] J. Nichols, *The Progresses, processions, and magnificent festivities of King James the First* . . . (1828), I, p. 559.

[4] P. Heylyn, *Cyprianus Anglicus* (1668), p. 53.

[5] *A Treatise of the Perpetual Visibility and the Succession of the True Church in All Ages.* When this was published in 1624, John Clare, a Roman priest, drew up an answer. It appeared as an Appendix to the author's *The Converted Jew or certain dialogues between Michaeas a Learned Jew, and others, touching divers points of Religion, controverted between Catholics and Protestants* (1630).

Rome but in "the noble worthies of the Christian world", among whom he numbered only the opponents of the Papacy, such as Wycliffe, Huss, Luther, Calvin, the Albigenses, and the Waldenses. It was they, he maintained, not the Church of Rome, who "after they had finished their course, delivered the lamp of their doctrine from one to another".[1] "That the Bishop of Rome, and his Pontifical Clergy, should have the face of the Church tied, and inseparably joined unto them, we can in no sort yield, but do disclaim it as a flattering tale."[2] Using the book of Revelation as his authority, Abbot affirmed that the Bishop of Rome is "the greatest Anti-Christ that ever yet was manifested among men". The Roman Church had ever been in apostasy, but there had always been those who feared God aright, and it was they who "do make up the universal militant Church".[3] Thus to the question: Where was our Church in former ages? answer must be made that it was in England, in France, in Spain, in Italy, even in Rome itself, among those who "loathed both the See of Rome and the whole courses of it".[4]

The following year Laud preached in St Mary's Church a sermon which was condemned by Abbot's successor as Vice-Chancellor, Dr Henry Airy, Provost of Queen's, "as containing in it sundry scandalous and *Popish* passages, the good man [i.e. Airy] taking all things to be matter of *Popery* which were not held forth unto him in *Calvin's Institutes*".[5] According to Heylyn, Abbot brought all his influence to bear against Laud. "He so violently persecuted the poor man, and so openly branded him for a *Papist,* or at least very *Popishly* inclined, that it was often made a *Heresy* (as I have heard from his own mouth) for any one to be seen in his company, and a *misprision* of *Heresy* to give him a civil Salutation as he walked the Streets."[6]

Thus began the feud which was to persist throughout Abbot's life, breaking into the open from time to time and in the end becoming an open struggle for power, in which Laud succeeded in "standing upon the higher ground, and more above him [i.e. Abbot] in respect of Power than beneath in Place".[7] Heylyn

[1] Op. cit., "To the Reader".
[2] Ibid., p. 3.
[3] Ibid., p. 20.
[4] Ibid., pp. 94, 97.
[5] Peter Heylyn, *Cyprianus Anglicus* (1668), p. 54.
[6] Ibid.
[7] Ibid.

asserted that every opportunity for preferment that came to Laud was scotched by Abbot, who so estranged the King from Laud that the latter "seeing his hopes more desperate than at the first . . . was upon the point of leaving the Court".[1] We may perhaps give Abbot the benefit of the doubt by assuming that his motive in opposing Laud so vehemently was—initially, at any rate—a sincere hatred of Laud's theological position as one which at all costs must be prevented from influencing the Church of England and undoing what Abbot believed the Reformation had achieved.

In the spring of 1600 Abbot unsuspectingly met the notorious Jesuit priest, John Gerard, after the latter's escape from the Tower in 1597. Gerard was visiting Thame Park, the home of Lady Agnes Wenman, and while he was sitting in the dining-room after dinner discussing religious matters with his hostess and her ladies-in-waiting a visitor was announced. "He was a Doctor of Divinity from Oxford and a well-known persecutor of Catholics. His name was Abbot."[2] After an exchange of courtesies Abbot began talking volubly, without the least suspicion that he was in the presence of the escaped Jesuit—for Gerard, on the entry of Abbot, had commenced to play cards with the ladies. Presently Abbot spoke of a piece of news from London concerning a Puritan who had thrown himself from a church tower and had left behind a note in which he claimed that he was certain of eternal salvation.[3] The following theological conversation ensued:

"Poor fellow," I [i.e. Gerard] said, "What could have induced him to destroy his body and soul in one fell act?"

"Sir," answered the doctor, in a learned and magisterial manner, "Sir, it is not for us to pass judgement on any man."

"Quite so," I said, "It is possible, of course, that the man repented of his sin as he was still falling, *inter pontem et fontem*, as they say. But it is very unlikely. The man's last act which we have means of judging was a mortal sin and merited damnation."

[1] Ibid. p. 65.

[2] *John Gerard: The Autobiography of an Elizabethan* (trans. Philip Caraman, 1951), p. 170.

[3] Dorrington, a wealthy Puritan, threw himself from the steeple of St Sepulchre's on 11 April 1600—*Sidney Papers,* II (ed. A. Collins, 1746), p. 187.

"But," said the doctor, "we don't know whether this was such a sin."

"Pardon me," I said, "it is not a case here of our judgement. It is a question of God's judgement; He forbids us under pain of hell to kill anyone, and particularly ourselves, for charity begins at home."

The good doctor was caught. He said nothing more on the point, but turned the subject, saying with a smile:

"Gentlemen should not dispute on theological questions."

"I agree," I said, "We don't, of course, pretend to know theology, but we should at least know the law of God, even if our profession is to play cards."

Shortly afterwards Abbot took his leave. "I don't know whether he left sooner than he intended", commented Gerard, "but I do know that we much preferred his room to his company."[1] It is clear that Gerard took a certain amount of gleeful delight in this exchange.

If Gerard's account of the discussion is correct and Abbot was somewhat shaky in his moral theology, there can be no doubt that he was no mean controversialist where Roman pretensions were concerned. In 1604 he published an attack upon "a certain audacious person who termeth himself Doctor Hill". Hill was a seminary priest who in 1600 had published a book entitled *A Quartron of reasons of Catholic Religion*, in which he had represented that the Roman faith was "the true faith of Christ", and that England was "a sink of wickedness beyond all the nations of the earth". This work was, in fact, a new version of a book by Richard Bristow[2]—what Abbot described as "a fresh garment made of other men's clothes". Abbot spent a year and a half preparing his reply to Dr Hill, being delayed first by his ordinary business and then by a fever which left him sick and weak for nine or ten weeks. Consequently, before Abbot's book was ready, a reply to Dr Hill by Francis Dillingham was published.[3] This

---

[1] Ibid., p. 171.

[2] *A Brief Treatise of divers plain and sure ways to find out the truth in this doubtful and dangerous time of Heresy. Containing sundry worthy motives unto the Catholic Faith* (1599).

[3] *A Quartron of Reasons, composed by Doctor Hill, unquartered, and proved a Quartron of follies* (1603).

spurred Abbot on to publish what he had already composed instead of delaying until the whole work was completed, which, in view of his many commitments ("I scant have been able to sustain the weight of the daily contingent and perpetually incumbent business"), might have taken a long time. The title of Abbot's reply, which was published in 1604, was *The Reasons which Doctor Hill hath brought for the upholding of Papistry, which is falsely termed the Catholic Religion, unmasked, and showed to be very weak, and upon examination most insufficient for that purpose.* This forthright composition of 438 pages was dedicated to his patron, Lord Buckhurst, and displayed considerable and varied learning, although, like most of the controversial writing of the period, it is a tedious work.

To Hill's charge that the Church of England was a divided Church and that it held within it several preachers holding different doctrines, Abbot replied that there are no

> differences of opinion in England, concerning the faith. Our Preachers do not differ, or teach diverse doctrines in any of their Sermons. We have for our rule the old and the new Testament, and the Confession of our Church in the Articles of Religion . . . and to these as to the Analogy of faith we do cleave, and there is no Graduate in our Universities, and much less, Preachers and Pastors in our Churches, but subscribe thereto. . . . The Religion which was then and is now established in England is drawn out of the fountains of the word of God and from the purest orders of the Primitive Church.[1]

This was indeed an idealized picture of the unanimity of preaching in the Church of England. Abbot appeared to have forgotten the efforts of the Puritan preachers within the Church of England who were constantly labouring to bring her doctrine and worship more into conformity with Calvinism, and to have ignored the rising influence of the opposing Arminianism, evidence of which had been much before him in his dealings with William Laud. It was certainly most misleading when Abbot added: "Such as you call Puritans did never differ from the rest in any part of substance but about circumstances and ceremonies, and about the manner of Ecclesiastical regiment."[2]

---

[1] *The Reasons . . . Unmasked,* p. 101. [2] Ibid.

Hill had adduced as an argument for the truth of Rome's claims the extent of the Papal influence and the vast number of Papists in the world. But, replied Abbot, it is no argument to say that what is largest spread is therefore most true. "Sound religion is not the worse when it is but in a few: and the multitude which do hold it, or the wide spreading thereof, cannot make the false to be otherwise."[1] Perhaps Hill's most audacious assertion was that the Papists taught no doctrine but such as was derived from the Bible. Abbot began his reply to this by referring to the Council of Trent[2] as "wickedly equalling and making of the same authority traditions of men with the written Scripture", and he continued:

> With the like reverence do you use it [i.e. Scripture] here, as it were casting it into an odd corner . . . skipping over it as the dogs in Egypt do by the river Nile where they dare not stand and drink but lap as they run, and run as they lap, for fear of the Crocodile. So when you come to the Scripture you will stand to nothing, but touch and go, for fear lest some thing should here start out, which should devour you and your Popery.[3]

In 1604 Abbot was appointed one of the forty-seven "learned men . . . for the translating of the Bible". The translators were divided into six "companies", two to meet in London, two in Oxford, and two in Cambridge. Abbot was a member of one of the Oxford Companies which had the task of translating the four Gospels, the Acts of the Apostles, and the book of Revelation. King James ordered the bishops to confer on the translators the next vacant benefice in their dioceses worth more than £20, and he requested them in the meantime to make gifts of money to the translators.[4] The work of translating must have occupied a great amount of Abbot's time, and progress on the whole project was much slower than had been anticipated, with the result that it was

[1] Ibid., p. 243.
[2] "The famousness of your Conventicle at Trent is famously to be laughed at. It was eighteen years in acting . . . now a piece and then a patch, interrupted and to it again . . . most base and beggarly it proved"—ibid., p. 339.
[3] Ibid.
[4] Richard Bancroft to the Bishops—Baker MSS. (in British Museum), M.m.1.   ff. 163–5.

not until 1611 that the agreed version was completed.[1] Its title was *The Holy Bible, containing the Old Testament and the New: Newly Translated out of the Original Tongues: and with the former Translations diligently compared and revised by his Majesty's special Commandment.* It was also *Appointed to be read in Churches.*

[1] For a full discussion of the subject see D. Daiches, *The King James Version of the English Bible* (1941).

3

"Blown over the Thames to Lambeth"

Honour hath three things in it: the vantage ground to do good; the approach to kings and principal persons; and the raising of a man's own fortunes. He that hath the best of these intentions, when he aspireth, is an honest man; and that prince that can discern of these intentions in another that aspireth, is a wise prince. Generally, let princes and states choose such ministers as are more sensible of duty than of rising; and such as love business rather upon conscience than upon bravery; and let them discern a busy nature from a willing mind.

FRANCIS BACON, *Essay: Of Ambition*

ABBOT'S PATRON, the Earl of Dorset, died in 1608, and on 26 May Abbot preached the sermon at his funeral in Westminster Abbey. "Never was there any Nobleman", he said, using the fulsome terms customary on such occasions, "who with more humble agonizing, with more feeling and affectionate gratefulness did entertain the favour of his Sovereign, than this honourable person did."[1] Abbot had the good fortune to find a new and even more influential patron in George Hume, first Earl of Dunbar. Dorset had been one of Queen Elizabeth's faithful counsellors whom James I had wisely retained, but Dunbar was a close personal friend who had accompanied James from Scotland to England, and has been described as "omnipresent with James, a prime favourite, his Majesty's very breath and spirit".[2] Chancellor of the Exchequer and Master of the Wardrobe, he was also the King's chief adviser and lieutenant for Scottish affairs, which loomed so large in the royal mind. In

[1] *Sermon Preached at Westminster, May 26, 1608, at the Funeral Solemnities of the Right Hon. Thomas Earl of Dorset* (1608). See also above, p. 15.
[2] D. H. Willson, *King James VI and I* (1956), p. 176.

thus attaching himself to Dunbar Abbot was automatically brought within the orbit of royal influence.

Not that Abbot was unknown to the King. In 1603 he had carried to the King at Woodstock the congratulations of the University on the occasion of his accession,[1] and had also contributed to the series of poems by members of the University which was compiled in honour of the same occasion.[2] Two years later the King paid a formal visit to Oxford, and Abbot, as Vice-Chancellor, was much in his company. As part of the official programme the King attended theological disputations in St Mary's Church, where the subjects for debate were the power of saints and angels to know the hearts of men and the duty of pastors to visit those infected by the plague. Abbot was moderator at these disputations.[3]

In 1606 he had received a singular mark of royal confidence. As Dean of Winchester he had a seat in the Convocation of Canterbury, and in that year both Houses formally approved the notorious *Convocation Book of John Overall*. This book consisted of chapters of theological explanation together with canons based upon them. It aimed at refuting the claims of Papal supremacy and the doctrine of secular government as propounded by the Jesuits and by the sectaries. It made large claims for the divine right of kingship and affirmed that "Subjection of Inferiors unto their Kings and Governors, is grounded upon the very Law of Nature". It asserted that even a usurped authority "is ever . . . to be reverenced and obeyed", and it was this claim which displeased King James, for such a doctrine of non-resistance would confirm every usurper in undisturbed possession of his throne and would forbid a nation going to the aid of a rightful King who returned to claim his throne. Consequently, the proposed canons never received the Royal Assent, and the book remained unpublished until 1689.[4] What was significant as a sign of Abbot's rising influence in royal circles was the fact that the

---

[1] *D.N.B.*, "Abbot, George".

[2] *Academiae Oxoniensis pietas erga serenissimum et potentissimum Iacobum Angliae Scotiae Franciae et Hiberniae Regem, fidei defensorem, Beatissimae Elisabethae nuper Reginae legitime et auspicatissime succedentem* (1603).

[3] C. E. Mallet, *History of the University of Oxford* (1924), II, p. 232.

[4] Published in that year by William Sancroft under the title *Concerning the Government of God's Catholic Church and the Kingdoms of the whole world.*

King's remonstrance on the subject was contained in a letter addressed to Abbot and partly written in his own hand.[1] "Good Dr Abbot," the letter began, "I cannot abstain to give you my judgement of your proceedings in your convocation, as you call it", and then the King proceeded to indicate the weakness of the doctrine of non-resistance to a usurping monarch. He advised Abbot to "meddle no more" with such theories, "for they are edge tools", and concluded, "I commit you to God's protection, good Dr Abbot, and rest Your good friend, JAMES R."

After being thus singled out as the repository for the royal views on a matter of some considerable importance it is not surprising that Abbot should reciprocate by describing the King as "the most religious, the most learned, the most judicious King, that this land ever enjoyed".[2] And now the occasion arose which was to prove to be an opportunity for him to serve the royal cause with such zeal that his feet were placed on the path which was to lead him rapidly to Lambeth.

For several years James I had endeavoured to restore power to the episcopate in Scotland,[3] and in 1600 he had appointed three diocesan bishops. As they had little authority the Presbyterian Kirk went on its way with unabated vigour. When he became King of England James determined to try again. He postponed a meeting of the General Assembly due in Aberdeen in 1604, but when a second postponement followed, nineteen ministers defied the royal order and unlawfully met. They were summoned to appear before the Council in Scotland, and James sent the Earl of Dunbar to secure a conviction. Largely as a result of the Earl's efforts the ministers were condemned. Thus James owed a debt of gratitude to Dunbar. In 1608 a General Assembly was summoned at Linlithgow to confer on the subject of episcopacy, and this time the Earl was accompanied by his chaplain,

---

[1] D. Wilkins, *Concilia Magnae Britanniae et Hiberniae* (1731), IV, p. 405; E. Cardwell, *Documentary Annals of the Reformed Church of England* (1839), I, p. 332.

[2] *Sermon Preached at the Funeral of the Earl of Dorset.*

[3] For the course taken by the Reformation in Scotland, see Gordon Donaldson, *The Scottish Reformation* (1960). Dr Donaldson conclusively disposes of the popular view that episcopacy was abolished in Scotland at the Reformation. "The office of bishop, although eclipsed, was not abolished in 1592, or at any point before 1638"—op. cit., p. 220.

George Abbot, whose specific task it was to put the claims of episcopacy before the Scottish ministers. He was well received by the Assembly,[1] and James received a letter from the Scottish bishops describing with enthusiasm the effects of Abbot's preaching.

> We cannot omit to show your Highness that Doctor Abbot had here an excellent sermon in presence of the Assembly, whereby he persuaded us mightily to peace and love towards others, which was well accepted, as he had public thanks accorded to him by the whole Assembly. . . . Our Assembly that in the beginning . . . [had] some great diversity in their votes ended with singing of the Psalm, *Ecce quam bonum et quam jocundum,* etc.[2]

That was not all, for Abbot advanced still further in the royal favour. Before his accession to the throne of England, an attempt had been made on James's life at the house of the Earl of Gowrie by the Earl's brother, Alexander, the Master of Ruthven, with the complicity of the Earl himself. The King had escaped and the Earl and his brother were slain. James then issued an official account of what had occurred, but the story contained so many inconsistencies that rumour spread that the King's version of the plot was not the true one and that the whole affair was a scheme of the King's to rid himself of the whole Gowrie house. This is unlikely, but so too was the royal version that the Gowries plotted to murder the King. In fact, it is possible that the whole thing emerged from a sudden quarrel.[3] Needless to say the King was very sensitive about the matter and when, in 1608, a Scots attorney, George Sprot, was arraigned for complicity in the conspiracy, gossip once again voiced its doubts. The trial was held while Abbot was in Scotland and he seized the opportunity to defend the King's version. He watched the proceedings against Sprot and attended him to the scaffold. Then he published a

---

[1] Sir William Bowyer to Salisbury, 2 Aug. 1608—*S.P. Dom. Jas. I*, xxxv, 36.

[2] Archbishop and Bishops of Scotland to King James I, 31 July 1608—*Original Letters relating to Ecclesiastical Affairs of Scotland,* ed. D. Laing (Bannatyne Club, I, 1851), p. 146.

[3] For a modern discussion of the problem, see D. H. Willson, *King James VI and I* (1956), pp. 127–9.

pamphlet[1] which consisted of notes taken by the judge at Sprot's trial, with a long Preface in which Abbot gave a full account of Sprot's execution and of the whole "treasonable device between John, Earl of Gowrie . . . plotted . . . for the cruel murdering of our most gracious sovereign". This defence of the King's version of the plot was published in London in order to convince those people in England who were still doubtful. In the course of his Preface Abbot expressed flattery of the King, describing him as one "whose life hath been so immaculate and unspotted in the world, so free from the touch of viciousness and straining imputation, that even malice itself, which leaveth nothing unsearched, could never find true blemish in it, nor cast probable aspersions on it".[2] He proceeded to compare King James with David, Solomon, Josiah, Constantine the Great, Moses, Hezekiah, and Theodosius. It is unlikely that this panegyric escaped the notice of James who was highly susceptible to flattery.

With this sturdy service to the King's cause to his credit Abbot then returned to England. He had earned the King's gratitude for his persuasion with the Scottish ministers and for his pamphlet on the Gowrie conspiracy. His praise of King James showed that he had the right idea about the royal person. His theological abilities were already known to the King. The influence of the Earl of Dunbar ensured that his reward would not be delayed. In the event his promotion was meteoric, for in a little over three years he was raised from the Deanery of Winchester to the Archbishopric of Canterbury. "He did first creep, then run, then fly into preferment." wrote Thomas Fuller,[3] "or rather preferment did fly upon him."

First, in May 1609, he was elected Bishop of Lichfield and Coventry, following the death of John Overall. He was not consecrated, however, until the beginning of December and he was enthroned on 29 December.[4] We know nothing of his episcopate,

---

[1] *The Examination, Arraignment and Conviction of George Sprot . . . written and set forth by Sir William Hart . . . Before which Treatise is also prefixed a Preface, written by G. Abbot, Doctor of Divinity, and Dean of Winchester, who was present at the said Sprot's execution* (1608).

[2] Pp. 34 f.

[3] *Worthies of England* (ed. J. Freeman, 1952), p. 552.

[4] J. Le Neve, *Fasti Ecclesiae Anglicanae* (1854), I, p. 556.

for there is a gap in the Episcopal Registers for the period covering Abbot's term of office. The only incident of which we have any knowledge is that in June 1609 he, together with the Archbishop and the Bishop of London, dined with Sir Thomas Bodley and "entreated the Archbishop and the other to bestow a prebend" upon Thomas James, the first Keeper of the Bodleian Library.[1]

Abbot had been Bishop of Lichfield for a mere nine months and in episcopal orders for only one when preferment was again bestowed upon him. Thomas Ravis, Bishop of London, died and rumour[2] that Abbot would be translated to this important see was confirmed when on 12 February 1610 he was enthroned as Bishop of London.[3] Shortly after his appointment he resigned the Mastership of University College, Oxford.[4]

During his London episcopate Abbot performed some eighty-three institutions to benefices and collations to canonries[5] and in November 1609 he held a Visitation of his diocese.[6] In August he consecrated a new churchyard which had been presented to St Bride's parish by the Earl of Dorset, the son of his late patron,[7] and in October he presided[8] at the consecration of Scottish bishops in the chapel of London House. By this date two archbishops and eleven bishops had been appointed for Scotland but they had not yet received consecration. Three of them were summoned to England to receive consecration at the hands of English bishops so that afterwards they might return to Scotland

[1] Sir Thomas Bodley to Thomas James, 16 June 1609—*Letters of Sir Thomas Bodley to Thomas James* (ed. G. W. Wheeler, 1926), p. 184.

[2] "Dr Abbot the Bishop of Lichfield is the likliest for the See of London" —Sir Thomas Edmondes to William Trumbull, 28 Dec. 1609—*Downshire MSS. 1605–10 (Hist. MSS. Reports,* Series 75 (2), p. 211).

[3] J. Le Neve, op. cit., II, p. 303; Guildhall Library MSS., 9531/13, f. 392.

[4] On 23 Feb.—*University College Register.*

[5] *Registers of Bishops of London*—Guildhall Library MSS., 9531/14, ff. 141–56.

[6] *Journal of House of Lords,* II, 10 Nov. 1609: "Absence of the Lord Bishop of *London* was by the Lord Chancellor excused, for that the said Lord Bishop is this Day necessarily elsewhere employed about his Visitation."

[7] R. Newcourt, *Repertorium Ecclesiasticum Parochiale Londinense* (1708–10), I, p. 316.

[8] In order to prevent any misconception that Scotland was being brought under English jurisdiction, neither Primate took part in the consecration.

to consecrate the rest. Abbot's co-consecrators were the Bishops of Ely, Rochester, and Worcester, and he no doubt regarded the service in the chapel of his London residence as in some sense the finishing touch to his work in Scotland two years before.[1]

While he was at London Abbot gained a reputation for indefatigable energy in his public duties and for piety and generosity in his private life. His letters to Lord Salisbury show that he repressed with a strong hand any signs of Romanism. In November 1610 he committed a London scrivener for harbouring certain books and papers,[2] in December he forwarded to Salisbury papers containing English intelligence which had been taken from a man who possessed popish books,[3] and in January 1611 he recommended to Sir Thomas Lake that a certain aged priest should be confined.[4]

Abbot took his seat in the House of Lords at the opening of the parliamentary session on 9 February 1610. The House sat almost daily until 23 July, and the diligence of Abbot's attendance is shown by the fact that he was absent on only three occasions,[5] while in the session which began on 16 October he was absent on only two occasions before his translation to Canterbury. Membership of the House brought Abbot into contact with an immense variety of business and during the time he was Bishop of London he sat on no less than forty-three Committees of the House. Some of these were concerned with religious and moral matters, such as non-residence and pluralities, scandalous and unworthy ministers, and ecclesiastical canons. Most of them, however, were of a very secular character, ranging over a diverse variety of matters, such as repairing the harbour at Minehead, the erection of "Common Brewhouses", the better maintenance of manual occupations, and the breeding of calves. He was a member of the Committee appointed to confer with the Lower House on the subject of the Great Contract, under which it was proposed that

---

[1] See J. S. Spottiswoode, *History of the Church of Scotland* (1655), pp. 514 ff; T. Hannan, "The Scottish Consecrations in London in 1610", in *Church Quarterly Review*, Jan. 1911; Paul A. Welsby, *Lancelot Andrewes*, pp. 183 f, 215.

[2] Abbot to Salisbury, 26 Nov. 1610—*S.P. Dom. Jas. I,* lviii, 39.

[3] Abbot to Salisbury, 1 Dec. 1610—ibid., 50.

[4] Abbot to Sir Thomas Lake, 5 Jan. 1611—op. cit., xl, 1.

[5] *Journals of the House of Lords,* III.

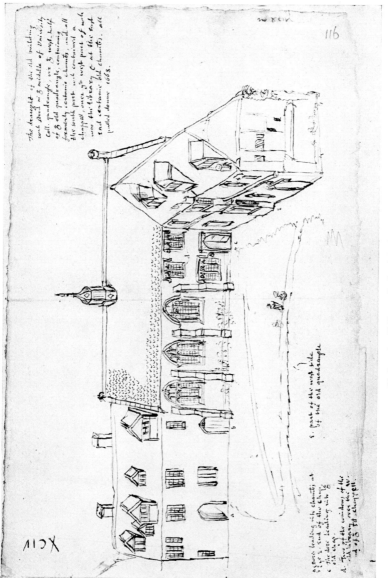

University College, Oxford, before 1663

Lambeth Palace in the seventeenth century

the King's financial difficulties and his subjects' grievances should be met by the King abandoning purveyances, wardship, and other feudal rights in return for an annual revenue of £200,000.

On 20 November 1610 Archbishop Richard Bancroft died. Immediately there arose the customary speculation about the identity of his successor. There were four bishops whose names were canvassed for the office—James Montague (Bath and Wells), Thomas Bilson (Winchester), Lancelot Andrewes (Ely), and George Abbot. The general opinion was that Lancelot Andrewes was the most suitable candidate and the one most likely to receive the appointment. Formerly Dean of Westminster and Bishop of Chichester, he stood high in the King's favour. A brilliant preacher, a learned theologian, and a staunch upholder of the divine right of kingship, he was on terms of personal friendship with the King, who appreciated good preaching, fancied himself as no mean theologian, and had an inflated conception of his royal office. Moreover, in 1608 James had published a defence[1] of the new and uncompromising oath of allegiance which had been imposed after the Gunpowder Plot and which the Pope had condemned as containing "many things contrarient to faith and salvation". An official reply was published by Cardinal Bellarmine,[2] and the King showed his confidence in Andrewes's learning and ability by entrusting him with the task of answering Bellarmine, which he accomplished[3] greatly to His Majesty's satisfaction. Thus, there was good reason for the confidence that he would go to Canterbury.

Peter Heylyn recorded that private consultations were held among some of the bishops and "other great men of the Court" to consider whom to recommend to the King. They felt unable to place any confidence in Montague or Abbot, "both of them being extremely popular and such as would ingratiate themselves with the *Puritan* Faction, how dearly soever the Church paid for it". They resolved to fix on Andrewes, "a man, as one says very well of him, of Primitive Antiquity, in which was to be found whatever is desireable in a Bishop . . . to whom they found the King

---

[1] *Triplici Nodo, Triplex Cuneus, or an Apology for the Oath of Allegiance.*
[2] *Responsio Matthaei Torti ad librum inscriptum, Triplici, etc.* (1608).
[3] *Tortura Torti* (1609).

to be well affected". According to Heylyn, the King received their recommendation warmly, and full of confidence they retired from the Court. But they had reckoned without the Earl of Dunbar. When they had gone into the country, the Earl went to the King and pleaded the cause of Abbot, reminding him no doubt of the bishop's service to the Crown in Scotland. Heylyn said that "he put it so powerfully in his behalf, that at the last he carried it, and had the King's Hand to the passing of the *Public Instruments*".[1] Whether the last statement was true or not, there was considerable delay before the appointment was publicly announced. During that time the Earl of Dunbar died[2] and to many this might have appeared to have altogether ruined Abbot's chances. In fact it merely strengthened the King's decision to appoint him, for he regarded it as a fitting act of respect to the memory of the dead Earl to whom he had owed so much. In February 1611 Abbot's appointment was announced and on the twenty-fifth of that month Sir Thomas Lake wrote to Lord Salisbury: "The King has chosen the Bishop of London to be Archbishop of Canterbury as being an able man, and recommended by Dunbar, whose memory is dear to his Majesty."[3] According to Secretary Calvert, the King told the Council and Abbot himself that

it is neither the respect of his learning, his wisdom, nor his sincerity (although he is well persuaded there is not any one of them wanting in him), that hath made him to prefer him before the rest of his fellows, but merely the recommendation of his faithful servant Dunbar that is dead, whose suit on behalf of the bishop he cannot forget, nor will not suffer to lose his intention.[4]

Thus the combination of the powerful influence of Dunbar, the ability displayed by Abbot himself in Scotland, and James's tendency to use ecclesiastical patronage to reward political service, brought George Abbot, Bishop of London, to the Primacy of Canterbury. "By a strong north wind coming out of Scotland,"

---

[1] P. Heylyn, *Cyprianus Anglicus* (1668), p. 63.
[2] 30 Jan. 1611.   [3] *S.P. Dom. Jas. I*, lxi, 107.
[4] George Calvert to Sir Thomas Edmondes, 10 March 1611—T. Birch, *Court and Times of James I* (1849), I, p. 110.

wrote Calvert, Abbot was "blown over the Thames to Lambeth."[1] It has been asserted that Abbot himself had no confidence that he would be appointed. "Preferment did fly upon him", wrote Fuller, "without his expectation."[2] In many ways, however, Abbot was more the type of archbishop that James wanted than were any of the other candidates. Like James, he was devoted to episcopacy, but—again like James, and unlike Lancelot Andrewes —his reason for this was utilitarian rather than theological, for both he and the King saw the office more as a Crown appointment than as a divinely necessary institution. Moreover, Abbot was a courtier and one whose interests were as much political as ecclesiastical. Finally, Abbot was a Calvinist without accepting all the Puritan implications,[3] and James, although it is doubtful how far he himself was a thoroughgoing Calvinist, no doubt regarded the appointment as a sop to the Puritans, particularly to those in Parliament, without opening the gates to their more radical aspirations.

The Church of England found itself with a new archbishop. Clarendon[4] was later to maintain that the appointment of Andrewes instead of Abbot would have stemmed the rising ride of Puritanism, and Peter Heylyn[5] considered that "if *Andrewes* had succeeded *Bancroft,* and *Laud* followed *Andrewes,* the Church would have been settled so sure on a Foundation that it could not easily have been shaken". Few people would now agree with their judgements, for Puritan feeling was so strong that it is arguable that the crisis, so far from being averted, might well have been precipitated if such had been the succession. Nevertheless Abbot's appointment had grave consequences for the Church and undoubtedly contributed to the troubles which were to come. His predecessor, Richard Bancroft, was one of the greatest ecclesiastical administrators. "He reformed abuses, recovered Church property, restored Church discipline and published the canons by which the Church of England is still ruled."[6] According

---

[1] Ibid.

[2] T. Fuller, *Worthies of England* (ed. J. Freeman, 1952), p. 552.

[3] See above, p. 7.

[4] *History of the Great Rebellion* (1717), I, p. 88.

[5] *Cyprianus Anglicus* (1668), pp. 63 f.

[6] H. Trevor-Roper, "King James and his Bishops", in *History Today,* Sept. 1955.

to Heylyn, when the other bishops heard of Abbot's appointment, they very much feared "that *Abbot* would unravel the Web which *Bancroft* with such pains had weaved".[1] Their fears were justified, for although Bancroft had achieved much, still more awaited to be done. Ignorance, non-residence, and pluralism were still rife among the clergy and their incomes were still inadequate; but, in spite of the fact that Bancroft's skilled administrators, such as Sir John Lamb, Sir Charles Caesar, and Sir John Bennett, became the backbone of Abbot's administration, a period of major reconstruction in the English Church came to an end, for, incapable of effective action in the second half of his primacy, Abbot failed to give the Church the ecclesiastical policy it so sorely needed. "The result of Abbot's translation marked a complete reversal of Bancroft's policy. A great administrator, a reformer of abuses, and a restorer of discipline was succeeded by a negligent, lax, and secular prelate."[2] Moreover, Bancroft had managed, through discipline, to weld into some semblance of unity the parties within the Church. Under Abbot, with the discipline relaxed, the Church began to slip back into its earlier confusion. The result of it all was that much of Bancroft's work was allowed to fall into ruins.

In the end the appointment pleased nobody. It was rumoured that Bishop Andrewes had said "that if York had it, it was but his right. If Winchester, that he had but his desert, but if London had it, then he had wrong."[3] The "high church" wing of Anglicanism, as represented by Andrewes and Laud, was forced to wait twenty-three years before it could take up Bancroft's work, and it is an interesting question how much of Laud's fiery intolerance as archbishop was due to frustration during the long primacy of Abbot. The parochial clergy urged the new archbishop's unfitness because, in view of the fact that "he was never incumbent in any living with cure of souls", he would lack sympathy with their trials and difficulties.[4] The Romanists knew

[1] *Cyprianus Anglicus* (1668), p. 63.

[2] Paul A. Welsby, *Lancelot Andrewes,* p. 112.

[3] William Devick to William Trumbull, March 1611—Downshire MSS. (*Hist. MSS. Comm. Reports,* Series 75 (4), p. 30).

[4] T. Fuller, *Worthies of England* (ed. J. Freeman, 1952), p. 552. But he knew their troubles well enough, if at second-hand—see above, p. 13.

they could expect no mercy from the new archbishop. "The Catholics complain bitterly", wrote the Venetian Ambassador in a dispatch containing the news of Abbot's appointment, "as he is held to be their bitterest persecutor."[1] The Puritans, who might have been expected to feel consoled by the appointment of a Calvinist, were very apprehensive, for they detected in Dunbar's influence a sign that the preferment was of a piece with the King's Scottish policy, and they soon raised an outcry against possible prelatical intolerance. The non-conforming Puritans had had their views expressed in a tract published before Bancroft's death, in which the publisher had written of his fears that those "whose conscience can not wholly yield to conformity required, shall be persecuted hereafter no less grievously than they have been heretofore. Especially if *D. Abbot* prove Archbishop of *Canterbury*."[2] Unwanted by both wings of his own Church, feared by sectaries and Romanists, his appointment pleased nobody but King James. Before many years had passed, the King too had had second thoughts.

[1] Marc' Antonio Correr, Venetian Ambassador, to the Doge and Senate, 17 March 1611—*S.P. Venetian,* xii, 189.

[2] *A Survey of the Book of Common Prayer,* by an anonymous author (2nd ed. 1610): "Publisher to the Reader".

4

"*The Archbishop's grave Interposing himself*"

A bishop may preach the Gospel more publicly and to far greater edification in a court of judicature, or at a Council-table, where great men are met together to draw things to an issue, than many preachers in their several charges can.

WILLIAM LAUD, Works

If any man be so addicted to his private, that he neglect the common, state, he is void of the sense of piety, and wisheth peace and happiness to himself in vain. For, whoever he be, he must live in the body of the Commonwealth and in the body of the Church.

Ibid.

ABBOT HAD been nominated to the See of Canterbury on 4 March 1611 and he was "very honourably installed at Lambeth" on 9 April,[1] upon which day he paid over £2,682 as the first instalment of first-fruits, the total payment of which was spread over four years. He was enthroned by proxy in Canterbury Cathedral on 16 May.[2] There is almost a complete absence of evidence concerning Abbot's diocesan work. His predecessors had spent the greater part of the summer at Canterbury, during which time they feasted the gentry, relieved the poor, and entertained their tenants. For some unknown reason, Abbot discontinued this practice. Instead, once or twice a year at the end of term

> he would cause enquiry to be made in *Westminster* Hall, the common Rendez-vous in St *Pauls* Church, and the Royal Ex-

---

[1] J. Nichols, *The Progresses, processions, and magnificent festivities of King James the First* (1828), II, p. 424 n; John Le Neve, *Fasti Ecclesiae Anglicanae* (1854), I, p. 26.

[2] Rawlinson MSS. (Bodleian Library), C. 155 ff.

change, for all such Gentlemen of his Diocese as lodged in and about the City of *London*, dispersing several Tickets from one to another, by which they were invited to a general entertainment at his house in Lambeth, the next day after the end of the present term where he feasted them with great bounty and familiarity. A course as acceptable to the *Kentish* Gentry as if he had kept open hospitality in his Palace at *Canterbury*; because it saved them both the trouble of attending on him, and the charge of sending Presents to him, both of which had been expected if he had spent any part of the year amongst them.[1]

For the three or four years preceding his death, however, he ceased to do even this, "fearing (as his affairs then stood) that it might render him obnoxious to some misconstructions, which he was willing to avoid".[2]

Abbot presented the Corporation of Canterbury with the city conduit which stood in the High Street. A dispute, however, arose about it between him and the Corporation, which was not to the Corporation's advantage. In his will Abbot stated that he had purposed to leave a yearly sum for the maintenance of the conduit, but "the mayor and corporation have used me so unrespectfully and ungratefully, that I have held fit to alter that purpose".[3]

Abbot held a Visitation of his diocese in 1629 and his Register at Lambeth Palace shows that he carried out a metropolitical Visitation between 1612 and 1616.[4] In addition he held *sede vacante* Visitations in a number of dioceses. There are several published copies of the Articles for the metropolitical Visitation,[5] which conform to the usual pattern of such documents. They supply evidence that, whatever Puritan theological opinions Abbot might hold, his public policy was to attempt to enforce good order in Church and parish. Careless and irreverent behaviour towards the altar, for example, which was encouraged by the

---

[1] P. Heylyn, *Cyprianus Anglicus* (1668), p. 242.   [2] Ibid.
[3] Abbot's Will, in *Life of George Abbot . . . Printed by J. Russell* (1777), p. 67.
[4] Abbot's Register (Lambeth Palace).
[5] E.g. *Articles to be inquired of, in the first Metropolitical Visitation of the most Revd Father, George . . . Archbishop of Canterbury . . . in, and for, the diocese of Lincoln, in the year of our Lord, 1613.* Other published versions have the same title, but leaving a blank for the name of the diocese.

more extreme Puritans within the Church, was by implication severely censured in the Visitation Articles. The question was asked whether there was

> a convenient and decent Communion Table, with a Carpet of Silk, or some other decent stuff, continually laid upon the Table at time of Divine Service, and a fair linen cloth upon the same, at the time of the receiving of the holy Communion . . . And whether it is so used out of Divine Service, as is not agreeable to the holy use of it: and by sitting on it, and by throwing Hats on it, writing on it, or is it abused to other profane uses?

Again, the Archbishop inquired whether the minister wore a surplice, whether he had admitted "offenders and schismatics" to Communion, whether he used the sign of the Cross at Baptism and the ring in Holy Matrimony. If the Minister was licensed to preach, did he preach regularly, in accordance with the canons, "standing and with his Hat off"? The Archbishop wanted to know on the one hand if the minister favoured recusants, instead of labouring diligently to reclaim them, and on the other hand if the minister endeavoured "to impeach or deprave the Book of Common Prayer or the Doctrine or Discipline of the Church of England". It is difficult to assess how far such Articles of Inquiry were effective, for it is not easy to trace the answers nor to measure the effectiveness of measures used to rectify abuses revealed by the answers.

When Richard Bancroft died he bequeathed his library to his successor and to "the Archbishops of Canterbury successively for ever".[1] Abbot willingly accepted responsibility for the library. He had a manuscript catalogue made of Bancroft's books, to which he wrote a preface declaring his intention of leaving his own library to the See on his death.[2]

If our knowledge of Abbot's purely ecclesiastical activities is scanty, there is every opportunity of observing his work and influence in national and international affairs. During the first two years of his primacy he was not without power in the councils of

[1] Ann Cox-Johnson, "Lambeth Palace Library, 1610–44", in *Transactions of the Cambridge Bibliographical Society* (1955), II, pp. 105 ff.

[2] See below, p. 145.

the State and in his influence with the King. He was a strong and eloquent advocate of the Church's rights in the controversy between the High Commission and the Common Law Judges, he was a useful ally to the King in the latter's interference in the Arminian struggle in Holland, and he had considerable influence on the course of the marriage negotiations which culminated in the marriage of Princess Elizabeth and the Elector Frederick of the Palatinate.

On 23 June 1611 Abbot was sworn a member of the Privy Council,[1] and occupation with affairs of the Council took up a considerable amount of his time. In 1613, for example, there were thirty meetings of the Council between May and September, and Abbot was present at twenty-seven of them, thus putting in an attendance higher than that of any other Councillor.[2]

Two months before he became a Councillor, Abbot had taken his seat on the High Commission, where he found himself in the thick of a long-standing legal conflict. By this time the High Commission, which had begun as a piece of administrative machinery for exercising the ecclesiastical supremacy of the Crown, had evolved into both a judicial court of first instance and an appellate tribunal.

Its penal jurisdiction penetrated to the most intimate details of the personal life of both clergy and laity, and it was used to repress vigorously any criticism of the royal supremacy. The main attacks against it revolved round its practice of inflicting fines and imprisonment (these being civil and not ecclesiastical penalties), the wide range of its jurisdiction, and the absence of any right of appeal from its decisions. . . . The Common Law Courts used as an instrument against the powers of the High Commission the ancient writ of prohibition, which had the effect of halting proceedings in any ecclesiastical court until

[1] Sir John Bennet to Sir Dudley Carleton, 15 July 1611—S.P. Dom. Jas. I, lxv, 32; John More to William Trumbull, 28 June 1611—Downshire MSS. (Hist. MSS. Comm. Reports, Series 75 (3), p. 99). Cf. Venetian Ambassador to the Doge and Senate, 21 July 1611 (S.P. Venetian, xii, no. 281): "The Archbishop of Canterbury is added to the Council, to its small satisfaction."

[2] E. R. Turner, The Privy Council of England in the Seventeenth and Eighteenth Centuries (1927), I, p. 98.

the Common Law Judges were satisfied that the matter fell within the jurisdiction of that Court.[1]

From 1607 onwards a veritable flood of prohibitions had constantly hindered the Commission's work. "The King and the Commission held the view that the Commission's proceedings were a proper exercise of the royal prerogative; the Common Law Judges, under the leadership of Coke, asserted that writs of prohibition, being part of Common Law, could not be altered by the King but by Parliament only."[2]

It was in the midst of this unresolved controversy that Abbot found himself. On 19 March 1611 the Commission committed Sir William Chancy to the Fleet for adultery and for refusing to support his wife. He obtained release from the Common Law Judges, who maintained that the Commission had no right to imprison for such an offence. Abbot appealed to the Privy Council against the Common Law Judges, and on 20 May Sir Edward Coke and the rest of the judges appeared before the Council to defend their conduct.[3] Most of the first day was occupied by Archbishop Abbot's charge against the judges. He described the latter's actions as abuses against God, against the King's government, against the Church, and against the Commonwealth. The Commission rested its case upon a statute of Elizabeth's reign, and the Common Law Judges had at that time found no fault with the power to fine and imprison. "In Coke's own report of Cawdry's case, he [i.e. Abbot] continued, the Commission was upheld as lawful, as having the power to fine and imprison, and as having jurisdiction over a long list of offences with which the Common Law might not deal, including most of those of which the Chief Justice now claimed jurisdiction."[4]

Coke began his reply the same day, but did not complete it until the next meeting on 23 May. During its course, Abbot interrupted to accuse Coke of evading the main point at issue, which was the nature of the power actually conferred by Statute. He further accused Coke of attempting "to overthrow, 'all upon

[1] Paul A. Welsby, *Lancelot Andrewes*, p. 220.   [2] Ibid.
[3] See R. G. Usher, *The Rise and Fall of the High Commission* (1913), pp. 212 ff; C. D. Bowen, *The Lion and the Throne* (1957), pp. 279 ff.
[4] R. G. Usher, op. cit., p. 214.

your own device', the ecclesiastical courts which had existed 'time out of mind'". Coke showed his indignation by answering that this "be the first time that ever any Judges of the Realm have been questioned for delivering their opinions in matter of laws according to their consciences in public and solemn arguments".[1] Abbot then briefly summed up the Commission's case, Coke followed with a summary of his own, and the proceedings ended. The Council was unconvinced by Coke and the judges, but the King promised that in the new Commission certain reforms would be made—a promise which was not fulfilled in the spirit in which it was received.

The judges of the Common Pleas were not informed of the contents of the new letters-patent, dated 29 August, but in October they were summoned to Lambeth Palace to hear the Commission read. They duly appeared in the Great Chamber of the Palace, but, although they found that their names were included in the number of the Commissioners, Coke and his colleagues refused to take their seats at the table until they had either seen or heard read a copy of the Commission. It was an awkward moment for Abbot, for he was eager to proceed. He had his programme carefully laid out, having "appointed divers causes of heresy, incest, and enormous crimes to be heard upon this day",[2] with the purpose of testing and confirming the Commissioners' new powers. Nevertheless he agreed that the Patent should be read. As soon as the judges heard it they realized that many of their complaints had not been met and that in some ways the Commission's authority was increased. The bishops and lords present then took the necessary oaths, but the judges refused either to take the oaths as Commissioners or to sit down, "fearing that the Archbishop would claim the victory unless they remained standing".[3] Abbot then "made an oration, describing the King's care for the peace of the Church, his desire for the extermination of heresy, and the creation of the Commission and its summary procedure to attain that end".[4] Next, he interrogated two heretics, in the hope that the judges might be convinced of the necessity of the Commission, but the judges remained standing,

---

[1] R. G. Usher, op. cit., p. 216.
[2] Ibid., p. 220.
[3] Ibid.
[4] Ibid., p. 221.

and finally the Court was adjourned, Abbot having promised the judges a copy of the Commission.

Neither side had won the battle. The High Commission continued its activities and the Common Law Judges continued to send out their writs of prohibition. Nevertheless Abbot had played a vigorous part in the Commission's defence against encroachments, and indeed had succeeded in increasing its authority. The consequences of this were to become apparent after his death when, under the presidency of Archbishop Laud, the Commission was to reach the height of its tyranny and unpopularity, thus paving the way for the Puritan hatred and overthrow of the Church of England.

If Coke was in disfavour for challenging the authority of the High Commission, the following year he was unpopular for asserting its authority. When, in that year, the trial and execution for heresy of Bartholomew Legate[1] and Edward Wightman were contemplated Coke maintained that the legal process should be through the High Commission. It was alleged that Legate was an Arian, who held that Christ was not God eternally and that to assert his divinity was blasphemy. He and Wightman had been brought before the Consistory Court of the diocese of London and had been committed to Newgate. James I proposed to make the case an example to the world of the orthodoxy of the Church of England.

Accordingly, on 21 January, Abbot wrote to Lord Chancellor Ellesmere, requesting him to appoint a Commission to deal with the case, emphasizing the King's anxiety to proceed against Legate. He urged the Chancellor to use great care in selecting judges "who make no doubt that the law is clear to burn them".[2] He suggested that Coke's name should be omitted from the commission, in view of his opinion that the case should come before the High Commission. He was convinced that Coke was wrong in holding this opinion, for he had consulted with "Mr Justice Williams . . . who maketh no doubt that the law is to burn them". In the event, Legate was burned at Smithfield and

[1] For the Legate Case, see W. Cobbett, *State Trials* (1809), II, pp. 727 ff; W. K. Jordan, *The Development of Religious Toleration in England, 1603–1640* (1932), pp. 43 ff.

[2] *Egerton Papers* (Camden Society, 1840), pp. 446–8.

a few days later Wightman, an ignorant and half-witted soul, perished in the same manner. These were the last two burnings for heresy in England, for a change was coming over both popular and official opinion. Up until now the torture and execution of heretics had been regarded as necessary and right, for only in this way (it was considered) was there hope that their sufferings might change their beliefs and thus save their souls. The eternal loss of the soul, which was regarded as the inevitable consequence of the deadly sin of false belief, was a greater evil than torture and execution, which might indeed produce salutary effects. As for George Abbot, he had already at Oxford quoted with approval St Thomas Aquinas's conclusion that, if need be, "men are to be enforced unto faith".[1]

Nevertheless, Abbot held that death should be the penalty for extreme forms of heresy only. In the autumn of 1612 John Jegon, Bishop of Norwich, wrote to Abbot about William Sayer who had been charged with certain Puritan and unorthodox views, among which may have been a denial of the divinity of Christ and of the Holy Ghost. Jegon had twice examined Sayer and, wishing to convict him, asked Abbot for authority to burn him. In his reply Abbot described Sayer as a heretic "who out of malice rather than understanding maintaineth many profane and schismatical opinions". The severe course of burning him, however, would "never be assented to" by ecclesiastical law, unless Sayer obstinately persisted in denying the divinity of Christ and of the Holy Ghost, in which case "the Law will take hold of him, as it did this year upon Legate and Wightman, to fry him at a Stake. But it is not clearly delivered what he affirmeth in these points, and therefore I can give no certain answer unto it."[2]

The chief reason for James I's eagerness to make the trial and burning of Legate an example of the orthodoxy of the Church of England was the controversy in which he was engaged with the Dutchman, Conrad Vorstius, who also held heretical opinions. Since 1579 Calvinism had become the established religion in

[1] See above, p. 14.
[2] Add. MSS. (British Museum), Mm.6. 58. f. 181; see C. Burrage, *The Early English Dissenters in the Light of Recent Research* (1912), I, p. 66; II, p. 170.

47

Holland and it was not prepared to tolerate diversity. When controversy did break out the country was split into two religious parties. The predominating party was Calvinist, professing a doctrine of strict predestination. The other was the Arminian (named after its leader Jacobus Arminius), "which modified the predestinarian doctrine by asserting the free-will of man and by speculating on the nature of God and on his relationship with man".[1] Into the details of the controversy, which bitterly divided Holland, there is no need to enter. James I was intensely interested and posed as the champion of orthodoxy against Arminian heresy. The violence of his views reached a climax when he openly interfered with the appointment to a post at Leyden University of Vorstius, who was a follower of Arminius.

Abbot wholeheartedly supported the King. He had already shown in his controversy with Laud at Oxford that Arminianism was abhorrent to him, for, in his judgement, it was a doctrine favourable to popery. In 1610 Petrus Bertius had published an Arminian work, entitled *Hymenaeus Desertor,* dedicated to all the ministers of the Gospel throughout Europe and vigorously attacking the Calvinist notion of the unconditional election of believers, whereby it is impossible for them to fall from grace. Although even his supporters considered the book to be too challenging, Bertius was rash enough to send a copy to Abbot. "Had you been advised by me," wrote Isaac Casaubon to Bertius, "you would never have sent your book to that prelate. He is a very religious man, but of the opposite opinion."[2] The following year, when it was proposed that Vorstius should be appointed to the professorship at Leyden, Sibrandus Lubertius of Franeker wrote to Protestant countries for help against the eternal foe. In a long letter addressed to Abbot on 21 August, he remorselessly exposed the errors of Vorstius,[3] although it is probable that Abbot had already perused Vorstius's *Tractatus Theologicus de Deo* and his *Exegesis Apologetica.*[4] The Archbishop passed on to the

---

[1] Paul A. Welsby, *Lancelot Andrewes,* p. 156.

[2] Simon Episcopus, *Praestantium ac eruditorum virorum epistolae ecclesiasticae . . .* (1660), no. 170.

[3] H. Rogge, *Jan Wtenbogaert* (1874–6), II, p. 109.

[4] R. Winwood, *Memorials of affairs of State in the reign of Queen Elizabeth and King James I* (ed. E. Sawyer, 1725), III, p. 296.

King Lubertius's exposures, together with his own views. James was enraged, drew up his own list of Vorstius's theological errors, and wrote to the British Ambassador at the Hague, Sir Ralph Winwood, instructing him to oppose the appointment of Vorstius.[1] Sir Ralph, in a letter to William Trumbull, noted the influence which Abbot had on the King, for—he wrote—the knowledge of Vorstius's errors "being come to the notice of our Lord of Canterbury, out of the care he hath to preserve religion in its ancient purity and integrity, he hath so far prevailed with his Majesty, that from him I have had charge publicly to protest against the reception of this Vorstius".[2] Vorstius himself was overwhelmed by these attacks and on 13 October he wrote to Abbot, humbly defending himself and begging Abbot to intercede with the King on his behalf. In the end, however, he was forced to retire from Leyden in 1612.[3]

One of the foremost of the Dutch Arminians was Hugo Grotius,[4] who visited England in 1613. Although the ostensible purpose of his visit was political and commercial, the real reason was to attempt to convert the King and as many ecclesiastics as possible to the Arminian point of view. Abbot had little patience with Grotius, and regarded him as an interfering busybody, "tedius and full of tittle-tattle", devoid of manners, and unreliable. In a letter which he wrote to Sir Ralph Winwood, who was now Secretary of State, Abbot warned him against Grotius and illustrated the latter's defects by describing his meeting with Grotius at a supper party given at Ely House by the Bishop of Ely, Lancelot Andrewes. Grotius had monopolized the conversation with a parade of learning, the Bishop of Ely meanwhile "sitting still at the supper all the while, and wondering what a Man he had there, who never being in his Place or Company before *could overwhelm them so with talk for so long a time*".[5] To show Winwood the true "Disposition of the Man", Abbot gave an account of what Grotius had done after the supper party. He had

[1] Ibid.   [2] Ibid.

[3] On this controversy, see A. W. Harrison, *The Beginnings of Arminianism* (1926), *Arminianism* (1937).

[4] On Grotius, see Charles Butler, *Life of Grotius* (1826); W. S. M. Knight, *Life and Works of Hugo Grotius* (1925).

[5] Abbot to Sir Ralph Winwood, 1 June 1613—R. Winwood, op. cit., III, p. 459.

requited Andrewes's hospitality by falsely reporting to the King Andrewes's views on the Arminian controversy and had asserted that Andrewes was himself an Arminian. The King had passed this on to Abbot and had expressed his displeasure that Andrewes should declare such opinions to a stranger. When Abbot had put the matter before Andrewes, the latter had stoutly denied that he had ever said these things to Grotius and he had offered to challenge Grotius. It was thus not without reason that Abbot warned Winwood against Grotius, neither was it the prejudiced opinion of a Calvinist with a personal dislike of Grotius, for this was not the only occasion upon which Grotius was guilty of misrepresentation.

The previous November (1612) Abbot had consented to be godfather to the son of Isaac Casaubon, another distinguished foreigner. Casaubon was a Frenchman by descent, whose religious opinions had been greatly influenced by his patristic studies. He had ceased to be able to accept extreme Calvinism, but on the other hand he was totally opposed to Roman Catholicism. He saw what he wanted in the non-Puritan wing of the Church of England, and in 1610 he had been invited by Archbishop Bancroft and others to visit England, where he finally settled. Abbot had no share in the invitation and after Bancroft's death Casaubon did not expect friendship from Abbot. In this he was mistaken for, in spite of the difference in their theological convictions, Abbot was always cordial to Casaubon, often sent for him to Lambeth, and made him a present each Christmas.[1] He aided with his influence Casaubon's endeavour to convert a Jew at Oxford, and he also read over Casaubon's attack on the *Annals of Baronius*.

There was harmony in the relations between the King and the Archbishop during these early years of Abbot's primacy. At Court he was treated cordially, even by the Queen who had no affection for his religious views. Prince Henry, who approved of his theology, regarded him with veneration. Among the officers of state he could count on the sympathy and friendship of the Earl of Salisbury, Lord Ellesmere, and Sir Ralph Winwood, while

[1] Mark Pattison, *Isaac Casaubon* (1892), p. 277.

a lavish hospitality at Lambeth secured him the support and favour of many. Nevertheless, he had his enemies, among whom Sir Robert Carr (Viscount Rochester), the Earl of Northampton, and Sir Edward Coke were chief. In fact the Court itself was split into two factions. On the one side there were the Howards and their dependants, chief among them being Henry Howard, Earl of Northampton, Thomas Howard, Earl of Suffolk, and Charles Howard, Earl of Nottingham, who were pro-Spanish and pro-Catholic. Against them was ranged a loose combination centred round men like Lord Ellesmere, the Earls of Pembroke and Southampton, and Sir Thomas Lake, who were anti-Spanish and Protestant. The former encouraged the King towards independence of Parliament, while the latter urged co-operation with Parliament. Archbishop Abbot ranged himself with the anti-Howard group and thus found himself on the side of the country as a whole, for since the time of the Spanish Armada the English mind had been possessed of a suffused and imprecise hostility towards Spain. The King inclined towards the Howard faction, and the bitter rivalry between the two groups was to dominate politics for years to come.

Abbot's religious views dictated his policy with regard to foreign affairs. He was accordingly hostile to Spain, wary towards France, and friendly to the Protestant powers. In 1611 and 1612 James's diplomacy centred on marriage arrangements for Prince Henry and Princess Elizabeth. At one stage it was proposed to marry Princess Elizabeth to the Duke of Savoy, brother-in-law to the King of Spain, a course which commended itself to the Earl of Northampton, who was a Papist and in secret correspondence with Spain. Abbot vehemently opposed it at the Council table, but it is unlikely that James would have pursued the proposal for he favoured Frederick, the Elector of the Palatinate, as a husband for Princess Elizabeth. In May 1612 the Elizabeth–Frederick marriage articles were signed, but a month later Spain sent a special ambassador, Pedro de Zuniga, to propose the King of Spain himself, now a widower, as a suitable husband for Princess Elizabeth. Abbot condemned the proposal and in a letter to the King he pointed out that the Ambassador had depended for the success of his mission upon members of the English Court who were susceptible to bribery and corruption. He had secretly dispensed £12,000 already in England and had also been in the country at the time of the Gunpowder Plot, and "God knows what share he had in that business."[1] Twelve days later Abbot again wrote to the King, informing him that de Zuniga had moved to the house of the Lieger Ambassador from France in order "that he may more freely transact his secret business".[2] The King was in an ill-humour and swore that his daughter should not marry a Papist, and so the Spanish proposals came to nothing. In the autumn the Elector Palatine came to England and in a short time he and the Archbishop were on friendly terms.

While these negotiations were proceeding, the Duke of Savoy had proposed a match between his daughter and Prince Henry. James was favourable to this marriage and Henry himself found that the beauty of his proposed bride and the determination of his father outweighed his religious scruples. Once again, Abbot opposed the match. On 9 October Giovanni Biondi told Sir Dudley Carleton that the Savoy match was nearly concluded and that all approved it except the Churchmen. He added: "The Archbishop of Canterbury has opposed it in vain".[3] These marriage proposals had been fully discussed in Council, where Abbot's chief antagonist had been the Earl of Northampton, Lord Privy Seal. It is interesting, therefore, that Chamberlain reported to Carleton on 26 November that several persons had been committed for reporting a difference at the Council table between the Archbishop of Canterbury and the Lord Privy Seal.[4]

Before either of the proposed marriages could take place Prince Henry died. He had been ill throughout the autumn and on 6 November his end came. During his last hours Abbot was constantly with him. "The Archbishop of Canterbury", wrote Chamberlain, "was twice or thrice with the Prince and dealt with him like a grave and religious churchman while he was in memory, and afterwards both prayed by him himself, and caused others to

---

[1] Abbot to the King, 22 July 1612—*S.P. Dom. Jas. I*, lxx, 11.

[2] Abbot to the King, 3 August 1612—ibid., lxx, 24.

[3] Giovanni Biondi to Sir Dudley Carleton, 9 Oct. 1612—*S.P. Dom. Jas. I*, lxxi, 12.

[4] Chamberlain to Carleton, 26 Nov. 1612—*S.P. Dom. Jas. I*, lxxi, 42.

continue in prayer while there was life."[1] When the Prince could no longer speak Abbot asked him to make a sign of his "faith and hope in the blessed resurrection" by "lifting up your hands". The sign was given and the Archbishop "with streams of tears, poured out at the bedside a most exeeding powerful passionate prayer".[2]

On 7 December the funeral took place and Abbot, "with grave sober countenance, showing the inward sorrow of his heart", preached a funeral sermon which lasted for two hours. His text was from Ps. 82.6–7: "I have said, Ye are gods; and so are all the children of the most Highest. But ye shall die like men: and fall like one of the princes." "He praised the loftiness of the Prince's ideas, and concluded by dwelling on the fragility of human life and hopes."[3]

Later that same month Princess Elizabeth and the Elector Frederick were officially betrothed by Abbot at Whitehall. John Chamberlain gave Carleton an amusing account of the ceremony. Sir Thomas Lake read the marriage contract, but his French was so bad that "it moved an unseasonable laughter as well in the contractors as the standers by, which was soon silenced by the Archbishop's grave interposing himself, and with an audible voice using these very words, 'The God of Abraham, Isaac, and Jacob bless these nuptials, and make them prosperous to these kingdoms and to his Church.'"[4] On 29 January 1613, in honour of the approaching wedding, Abbot gave a banquet for the Elector's suite. Frederick took this so kindly that just as the meal was about to begin he arrived himself, although he had not been invited. "The Entertainment was very great, and such as became the giver and receiver."[5] The Elector returned the hospitality by inviting the Council to feast at Essex House,

[1] Chamberlain to Carleton, 12 Nov. 1612—McClure, I, p. 389.

[2] J. Nichols, *Progresses*, II, p. 485; cf. also "The Life and Death . . . of Prince Henry", in *Collection of Scarce and Valuable Tracts* (*Somers Tracts*: ed. W. Scott, 1809–15), II, p. 241.

[3] Venetian Ambassador to the Doge and Senate, 29 Dec. 1612—*S.P. Venetian*, xii, no. 727; cf. also "Life and Death of . . . Prince Henry" in *Somers Tracts*, II, p. 247.

[4] Chamberlain to Carleton, 31 Dec. 1612—McClure, I, p. 399.

[5] Nichols, *Progresses*, II, p. 517.

where "he showed [Abbot] more kindness than to all the rest put together".[1]

The marriage was solemnized in the Chapel Royal on 14 February. The Bishop of Bath and Wells preached and "the Archbishop performed the other rites and ceremonies upon a stage raised in the midst of the chapel".[2] Before his departure from England the Elector made Abbot a present of a piece of plate valued at £1,000 as a mark of his appreciation for what Abbot had done to forward the marriage.

This period of Abbot's primacy may be conveniently concluded by turning to a few matters of a different character. Abbot had a share in founding the London Charterhouse as a hospital and school. He was among the first governors appointed by Thomas Sutton on 22 June 1611, and when Sutton died in December Abbot and the Bishop of Ely (Andrewes) were overseers of his will. The following year the will was challenged by Sutton's nephew and although the latter had no case, Francis Bacon supported him because he wished the benefaction to be diverted to channels more profitable to the King. Abbot was strongly opposed to such an act of injustice, and in the end his counsels prevailed. On 7 July 1613 Abbot, together with the Lord Privy Seal, went to Charterhouse "to take possession, and consult of the ordering and disposing of that great work".[3]

As Archbishop of Canterbury Abbot was Visitor of All Souls College, Oxford, and in this office he "soon made himself conspicuous for his opposition to the joviality of the age; and certainly spared no pains to make his position clear at All Souls on the point of repression and restraint".[4] His constant correspondence with the college reveals two predominating concerns. The first was the desire to preserve the college finances and to curb expenditure, and the second was a determination to enforce discipline.[5]

---

[1] Chamberlain to Carleton, 4 Feb. 1613—*S.P. Dom. Jas. I,* lxxii, 23.

[2] Chamberlain to Sir Ralph Winwood, 23 Feb. 1613—McClure, I, p. 427; cf. also Chamberlain to Alice Carleton, 18 Feb. 1613—McClure, I, p. 424.

[3] Chamberlain to Carleton, 8 July 1613—McClure, I, p. 463.

[4] M. Burrows, *Worthies of All Souls* (1874), p. 125.

[5] See, e.g., C. T. Martin, *Catalogue of the Archives in All Souls* (1877), pp. 310, 325.

Abbot was also Chancellor of Trinity College, Dublin. When James Ussher was in London in 1613 he had frequent conferences with Abbot about a new charter and statutes for Trinity College. In a letter to Dr Chaloner, Ussher stated the various criticisms which Abbot had made of the prevailing situation at Trinity College, and he picked out one "which could not be expected from such a quarter".[1] Abbot had "observed that there was no order taken that the Scholars should come into chapel *clericaliter vestiti*."[2] It was probably at this time that Abbot addressed a letter to Archbishop Jones, Lord Chancellor of Ireland, complaining that

> at the cathedral church in Dublin, as also at the College, the Prebendaries and dignitaries of the one, and the Provost and fellows of the other do refuse to come into the quire or into the the chapel on Sundays and Holydays in their surplices and hoods fit for their degree. I cannot express to your Lordship how exceedingly his Majesty is offended thereat.

The King, accordingly—added Abbot—orders the Lord Chancellor to call all those concerned before him to conform themselves to the laws and decent orders of the realm, or that they leave their places to such as will observe them.[3] About this time William Temple was appointed Provost of Trinity College and, having strong Puritan tendencies, he resisted Abbot's order to wear the surplice. When, after a term of disputes and mismanagement, Temple was persuaded to resign in 1626, Abbot supported Ussher's nomination of Mr Sibbes, Preacher of Gray's Inn.[4] Although Sibbes was elected, he declined the appointment because he had just accepted the Mastership of Katherine Hall, Cambridge, an office which he could hold along with the Preachership of Gray's Inn. The appointment went to Mr Bedel, who was another nominee of Ussher's. Writing to the "Seniors and other Fellows" of Trinity College on 2 June 1627 Abbot referred to "the distractions of your election, that for all the time your

---

[1] C. R. Elrington, *The Life of James Ussher* (1848), p. 37.

[2] James Ussher to Dr Chaloner—Elrington, op. cit., p. 37, quoting Ussher, *Works*, xv, p. 72.

[3] Abbot to Archbishop Jones, 25 Feb. 1613—Elrington, op. cit., p. 32.

[4] Richard Parr, *Life of James Ussher* (1687), pp. 374, 380.

college hath been forced to be without the principal governor thereof", and asked them to show all reverence and respect to the new Provost.[1]

At the beginning of 1613 Abbot's reputation was high. Unloved though he was by most sections of ecclesiastical opinion, he had done nothing to raise alarm, apart from his championship of the High Commission—where, however, he was acting in concert with other bishops. His attitude towards the burning of Legate did not appear to increase his unpopularity. His enemies at Court were unable to discredit him, for he had the support of the King. There had been minor differences between him and James, over the proposed marriage of Prince Henry into the House of Savoy and over Sutton's will. This, however, was outweighed by the Archbishop's support of James's theological interference in Holland, and by his championship of the marriage between Princess Elizabeth and the Elector Palatine. But the time was at hand when the royal approval was to give place to the royal displeasure.

[1] Elrington, op. cit., p. 86.

5

"I Doubt not but to Batter this Nullity to Dust"

Suspicions among thoughts are like bats amongst birds, they ever fly by twilight. Certainly they are to be repressed, or at least well guarded: but they cloud the mind; they leese friends; and they check with business, whereby business cannot go on currently and constantly. They dispose kings to tyranny, husbands to jealousy, wise men to irresolution and melancholy.

FRANCIS BACON, *Essay: Of Suspicion*

THE YEAR 1613 had opened auspiciously for Archbishop Abbot. The marriage of Princess Elizabeth to the Elector Frederick represented the triumph of his anti-Spanish policy against that of the Howards, who would have preferred a Spanish or Savoy match. The death of Prince Henry had put an end to the other marriage proposal to which he had been opposed. During the first five months of the year the Archbishop pursued the even tenor of his way. On Wednesday 19 April, he confirmed Prince Charles in the Chapel Royal in the presence of the King and Queen.[1] Then, on 12 May he had an interview with the King which marked the beginning of a series of events which were to be of the gravest consequence for him and which left him detested by the Howards, unpopular with the King, and admired in those quarters where hitherto he had never found popularity. The King requested him to be a Commissioner in the forthcoming case of the divorce of the Earl and Countess of Essex.[2]

In 1606 King James had given his approval of the marriage of

[1] For a full account of the case and the events leading up to it, see S. R. Gardiner, *History of England, 1603–42* (1883–4), II, ch. 16; W. McElwee, *The Murder of Sir Thomas Overbury* (1952), *passim.*

[2] Nichols, *Progresses,* II, p. 626.

Lady Frances Howard, daughter of the Earl of Suffolk, to Lord Robert Devereux, Earl of Essex. At the time of the marriage the bride was thirteen and the bridegroom fourteen. Immediately after the marriage the Earl went abroad to serve in the Netherlands and the Countess remained at Court where she became infatuated with the King's favourite, Robert Carr, Viscount Rochester. She was determined to marry Rochester and when her husband returned home at the end of 1609 and took her to his country house in Staffordshire, she used every artifice, including the administration of drugs and the practice of witchcraft, to prevent the consummation of the marriage. For three years this continued and it then became clear that she intended to sue for a nullity of the marriage. Essex, for his part, agreed to allow his wife to proceed, but with the condition that he would not make any admission reflecting upon his physical capacity, except in so far as the Countess was concerned.

When the King spoke to the Archbishop on 12 May,[1] Abbot requested that other bishops should be joined with him. The King assented to this and named the Bishops of London (John King), Ely (Lancelot Andrewes), and Lichfield and Coventry (Richard Neile). James raised no objection to Abbot's other request that he might speak privately with the Earl of Essex. The next day, therefore, the Archbishop sent for the Earl and, although he found him somewhat reserved, he was left in no doubt that Essex avowed "the ability of himself for generation; and that he was resolved never to lay any blemish upon himself that way".[2]

On 16 May the Divorce Commission was appointed.[3] It consisted of the Archbishop, the three bishops already named by the King, and six laymen (Thomas Parry, Julius Caesar, Daniel

---

[1] For the process of the trial and for Abbot's part in it we are dependent upon the official summary of evidence and verdict in W. Cobbett, *Complete Collection of State Trials* (1809), II, pp. 785 ff, and on a document attached to this summary, entitled: "The Following Account, written by Dr George Abbot, Archbishop of Canterbury, with the Speech he intended to have made, and King James's Letter to him, will throw much light upon that affair, and help greatly to explain it"—Sloane MSS. (British Museum), 3828, f. 6 ff. This "Account" was completed on 21 Oct. 1613, eight days after the end of the case, and the authenticity of the document has never been disputed. In the following pages it will be cited as *Account*.

[2] *Account*, p. 806.   [3] *S.P. Dom. Jas. I*, lxii, 133.

Dunne, John Bennett, Thomas Edwards, and Francis James), and on 2 June it met for its first session behind closed doors at Lambeth Palace. Lady Essex's petition and libel were heard and most members of the Commission were surprised to find that instead of asserting the Earl's general disability, it contained the plea *impotentia versus hanc*. Abbot, when he heard this, told the Countess's counsel that "they had laid a very narrow bridge for themselves to go over".[1] A number of his fellow-Commissioners agreed with him, although the Bishop of Ely, Lancelot Andrewes, remained silent—as he did throughout most of the trial, much to Abbot's astonishment.[2]

The Commission proceeded to hear witnesses, and evidence of no very decisive nature was taken from servants and acquaintances of the parties. When Essex himself was called to answer his wife's libel his replies were reluctant and inconclusive. It soon became clear to the Commissioners, and to Abbot in particular, that this was a case, not of impotency, but of lack of love between the parties. The Earl had said, "When I came out of France I loved her, but I do not so now, neither ever shall"—a statement upon which Abbot later commented that "it was want of love, and not any impotency; it was *defectus voluntatis* and not *defectus potestatis*".[3] Moreover, the Earl had stated that, while in general he had no impediment, he had never carnally known the Countess, but he laid the blame for this on the Countess herself, alleging that she had persistently refused him. This admission was damaging to the Countess's case, for it indicated a wilful refusal to consummate on the part of the Countess, and this has never, until modern times, been a ground of nullity.[4]

In order to meet the uneasiness aroused by these admissions,

---

[1] *Account*, p. 806.

[2] For a full account of Andrewes's part in the trial and for an assessment of his motives, see Paul A. Welsby, *Lancelot Andrewes*, pp. 235 ff.

[3] *Account*, p. 854.

[4] It should, perhaps, be explained that the modern distinction between the terms "divorce" and "nullity" did not then exist. In cases of adultery and cruelty the Court pronounced a decree of Separation, but the marriage tie remained. This was *divortium a mensa et thoro*. In cases of nullity, the Court declared the parties never to have been married and therefore each was free to marry again. This was *divortium a vinculo*. Thus the term "divorce" was applied to both.

the Countess's lawyers attempted to bolster up their case by suggesting that the Earl had been bewitched and that, as a result, he was *maleficiatus*, rather than *frigidatus, versus hanc*. No proofs were offered, however, and Abbot adjourned the Commission for a fortnight. It became clear that the chief obstacle to a quick settlement would be the Archbishop himself: for he was determined to sift the whole case conscientiously and to reach a true and considered judgement. The Countess's supporters, on the other hand, were anxious that the case should be disposed of as soon and as quietly as possible and without too much scrutiny of the evidence.

Some of the Howard faction went to the King to complain about the Archbishop. James, who was in possession of only part of the facts, was wholly on the Countess's side, and when he heard that the petitioners were encountering difficulties, he sent for the Archbishop on 24 June and passed the complaints on to him. Abbot denied their foundation and apparently satisfied the King. Before he left, James said something vague about wishing well to the nullity, but—the Archbishop noted—"so obscurely, that I did not conceive that earnestly he desired it".[1] After this unsuccessful approach to the King, the Howards continued their pressure against the Archbishop. Among the threats used was that Archbishop Grindal had been overthrown for not giving consent to the divorce of Dr Julio (which was not correct), the implication being that the same fate would overtake Abbot.

Early in July the Commission reassembled to consider the Earl's answer to the libel. Abbot sent the King a copy of the proceedings, and received from His Majesty "a letter written all with his majesty's own hand, showing dislike thereof".[2] It was agreed that the answers should be withdrawn, but later they were received again in an acceptable form, although they represented merely an acquiescence in the articles of the Countess's libel. Counsel for both sides made their submissions and then the divisions of opinion on the Commission itself began to emerge. There was a discussion about the lawfulness of the plea of *maleficiatus versus hanc,* and whether, even if it was admissible, the present case would come within the definition. The Bishop of

---

[1] *Account*, p. 809.　　　　[2] Ibid., p. 810.

London and Abbot himself expressed their doubts. Sir Julius Caesar, Sir Daniel Dunne, and Sir Thomas Parry were satisfied with the lawfulness of the plea, but even they required further evidence in the present case. They proposed that the Countess should undergo a physical examination. Abbot agreed, reluctantly, for he anticipated that little convincing evidence would be forthcoming. Four noble ladies, to be assisted by two midwives, were appointed for the purpose and in due course they reported in favour of the Countess. The Countess took a formal oath of the truth of all her proceedings and seven of her kinswomen confirmed her statements. Abbot was very sceptical. He believed that the midwives had been tampered with and "he was not impressed with the oath of the seven kinswomen; he had private information that one of them, Lady Knyvet, had wept for a whole day when she had been unable to refuse to appear; and another was Mrs Neile, wife of his colleague the Bishop of Lichfield who was known to be the most time-serving bishop on the bench and was now coming out openly for the divorce".[1]

Turning to the question of the sentence to be given by the Commission, Sir Daniel Dunne suggested that it should be given in general terms, without naming any particular impotency, but Abbot argued that public opinion would expect the Commissioners to state reasons for their decision. Sir Daniel said that a judge was not bound to give a reason for his judgement, but Abbot replied that even if a reason was not to be given publicly "is it not fit that I who am the judge, and must pronounce the sentence, know the grounds of that which I am to pronounce?" It was essential that he should know the reason for the sentence, "for as soon as this cause is sentenced, every man who is discontented with his wife, and every woman discontented with her husband, which can have any reasonable pretence, will repair to me for such nullities. . . . If I repel them I must show a reason."[2] When Abbot declared that there was no precedent in England for the annulment of a marriage on the ground of the husband's impotency towards his wife only, Sir Daniel Dunne cited the case of John Bury, whose marriage in the sixteenth century had

---

[1] William McElwee, *The Murder of Sir Thomas Overbury* (1952), p. 108.
[2] *Account*, pp. 811 f.

been annulled on the plea of impotence and who had then married again and had had children. This, Sir Daniel argued, was obviously a case of nullity on the grounds of impotence towards one woman. Abbot found this precedent "dishonestly drawn", because the annulment in Bury's case was on the ground of incapacity due to physical deformity following an accident, which made it impossible to believe that he was other than permanently impotent. Thus it was no case of *versus hanc*. Abbot also pointed out that although Bury had indeed married again and had children, when, after his death, there was some question about his estates, the lawyers declared that in view of his later capacity the former annulment was void and the first marriage stood. The Bury case was thus in fact a precedent *against* an annulment in the Essex case.

The situation was given a new development by a summons from the King to all the Commissioners to meet him at Windsor. James's object was to persuade the Commissioners to pronounce a divorce, and down at Windsor he reasoned with the dissentient or hesitant Commissioners, with the result that some of them, including Neile, Andrewes, and Parry, dropped their opposition. When the case was fully discussed in the King's presence, Sir Daniel Dunne insisted that Essex was *non potuit* to have intercourse with the Countess, but Abbot objected that the Earl's evidence showed that "the *Non potuit* was from lack of love and not for want of ability",[1] and he attacked Sir Daniel for giving the King a false account of the proceedings and for citing doubtful precedents. "Amongst us", he added, "was divers ways showed the insufficiency of the proofs; that the libel was laid short of the cause, and the proofs were short of the libel."[2] Sir Daniel, no doubt anticipating the rage of the Howards, said that if the divorce failed to go through, what a disgrace it would be to the Lord Chamberlain and his daughter. Abbot made the obvious answer that the parties should have considered that possibility before they embarked upon the proceedings. "Must I, to save any man from disgrace, send my soul unto hell, to give a sentence whereof I saw no good? I will never do it." The King spoke of some of the rumours about Essex which the Howards had passed on to him,

[1] Ibid., p. 813.   [2] Ibid.

but Abbot's only comment was: "I would to God we might see all these things proved." When the King showed how much in earnest he was that the divorce should go through, Abbot fell on his knees and begged with tears to be removed from the Commission. "I had said before, That I was the unfittest man that might be, to judge of such a cause; I was no married man, I was no lawyer."[1]

It was clear that the King was shaken, but not so much by the moral factors in the case as by the fear that, because of the stand being adopted by the Archbishop and the Bishop of London, the Commissioners would not do his will. After the meeting broke up, however, James was gracious to Abbot, and at dinner that day Sir Julius Caesar told him that the King found no fault in him. Nevertheless the rumour soon spread that the Archbishop was in disgrace and that he and the Bishop of London "should be hereafter kept to their spiritualities, and should meddle no more in temporal matters".[2]

Abbot fully realized the gravity of his position, and as he was being driven in his coach from Windsor to Lambeth and during the sleepless night that followed two things were much in his mind. The first was "what a strange and fearful thing it was that his Majesty should be so far engaged in that business; that he should profess that himself had set the matter in that course of judgement; that the judges should be dealt with beforehand, and, in a sort, directed what they should determine".[3] The second thing which troubled him was that in all the debating "we had all this while . . . never, or very little meddled with points of divinity".[4] In order to clarify his own mind on "points of divinity", he rose early and wrote out his views on the theological issues involved. The resulting paper[5] dealt only with the plea *maleficiatus versus hanc,* and Abbot maintained that neither the Scriptures, nor the Fathers, nor the Councils gave any warrant for a nullity of marriage on such a plea. The proper remedies for such a condition were alms, fasting, prayer, and medical attention, but

---

[1] Ibid., p. 813; cf. Revd Thomas Lorkin to Sir Thomas Puckering, 29 August 1613—T. Birch, *Court and Times of James I* (1849), I, p. 269.

[2] *Account*, p. 815.   [3] Ibid., p. 815.   [4] Ibid.

[5] "The Lord Archbishop of Canterbury's REASONS against the Nullity", in W. Cobbett, *Complete Collection of State Trials,* 1809, II, pp. 794 ff.

none of these had been applied in the present case. Instead, "the first hearing must be to pronounce a nullity in the marriage". The Archbishop later sent a copy of the paper to the King.

The next day the Commissioners met again at Lambeth and Abbot's "reasons of divinity" were discussed. No satisfactory conclusion was reached and Abbot was particularly distressed at Bishop Andrewes's unco-operative attitude, for "my Lord of Ely sat little less than dumb, as if he had never dreamed of any such matter", so that even "divers of the Commissioners wondered at him; that he who had spent so much time in reading of the canonists touching this question, should not think upon divinity".[1] Towards evening, Abbot expressed a wish that some effort should be made to bring about a reconciliation between the Earl and the Countess, but Bishop Andrewes "spake home about this, much disliking that any such thing should be sought; that it was too late; that it might be the cause of poisoning and destroying of one another to bring them together again".[2] In saying this Andrewes was more realistic than Abbot, for in the circumstances reconciliation was a council of perfection, although Abbot had the insight to know the real grounds for Andrewes's pessimism—it was because the separation was "so demanded and expected there is little chance of reconciliation".[3] By now it was certain that the vote of the Commissioners would result in a tie. Consequently the proper course would have been either to abandon the suit or to order a fresh hearing before a new Commission. The King did neither. Instead, he ordered the Commission to adjourn until 18 September and announced his intention of appointing two more Commissioners. The new members were to be Bishop Bilson of Winchester and Bishop Buckeridge of Rochester, both of whom the King knew to be compliant.

During the recess Abbot spent his leisure pondering the situation, reading all he could about the issues involved, and discussing the case with numerous people. Again and again he read through the depositions. He prayed long and earnestly for guidance. In the meantime rumour reached his ears that "a new husband was already provided" for the Countess.[4] He was in a

---

[1] *Account*, p. 817.   [2] Ibid.   [3] Ibid.
[4] Ibid., p. 819.

state of "expectation of some great discontentment". He had been informed that the King had carefully considered his "points of divinity" and that he had been observed busily writing during the interval between dinner and hunting. It was believed that he was composing a sharp letter in reply to the Archbishop. For the moment, however, the King remained amiable, sending Abbot his warrants for three bucks as he had always done. A few days before the Commission was due to meet, the King "did not only look merrily upon" him, but even went so far as to promise him the Bishopric of Lincoln for his brother, Robert.

Then the blow fell. On the evening of Friday 17 September the day before the Commission was to meet, Abbot was at his house at Croydon when the Bishop of Lichfield and Coventry (Richard Neile), who was an unreliable and scheming colleague, brought to him from the King a packet of papers. When he opened it he found his own paper against the nullity and with it the King's answer and a letter from the King, both written in the royal hand. The answer to Abbot's objections was a lengthy 3,000 word essay,[1] in which each of the Archbishop's "points of divinity" was dealt with in great detail. What the King's answer amounted to was that to say, as Abbot had, that the Scriptures, the Fathers, and the Councils could decide all controversies was preposterous, and Abbot ought to be satisfied that they said nothing positively *against* a nullity on the present grounds. The King suggested that the reason why *maleficiatus versus hanc* received no mention in these sources was because it was a devil's trick which had not then been discovered.

It is clear that throughout the case Abbot had the courage to remain loyal to his conscience. Unfortunately, in his correspondence with the King he played his cards badly and got submerged in theological arguments, instead of arguing on the facts of the actual case before him. It is to be noted that in the correspondence the debate was on whether *maleficiatus versus hanc* was, according to divinity, a sufficient ground for nullity. The fundamental question whether the Earl was in fact *maleficiatus versus hanc* or not was never even touched on. James I was quite prepared to

[1] The text is given in W. Cobbett, *Complete Collection of State Trials* (1809), pp. 798 f; based on Sloane MSS. (British Museum), 3828, ff. 2–5 and Harleian MSS. (British Museum), 813, f. 133.

discuss "matters of divinity" indefinitely and Abbot ought to have known that such discussion would get him nowhere. What he should have concentrated upon was evidence and facts, for the strength of his opposition rested there, and he should have attempted to convince James that those were very different from what the Howards had asked him to believe. His "points of divinity" appeared to the King to be irrelevant in view of the facts as James had received them. Abbot made no attempt to convince him that his knowledge of the facts was erroneous and so it was not unnatural that the royal essay in theology should be accompanied by a sharp letter[1] rebuking Abbot for wasting the King's time with trivialities. He accused the Archbishop of prejudice against the Countess, and asserted his own impartiality. He asked Abbot

> to have a kind of faith implicit in my judgement, as well as in respect of some skill I have in divinity, as also that I hope no man doubts of the uprightness of my conscience; and the best thankfulness that you that are so far my creature, can use towards me, is, to reverence and follow my judgement, and not to contradict it, except where you may demonstrate unto me that I am mistaken or wrong informed.

In spite of the eulogies he had made in the past about kingship in general and King James in particular, Abbot—unlike Andrewes—remained unimpressed by this bland assertion of royal superiority and infallibility.

Nevertheless, the Archbishop was very disturbed. After he had retired to his study and had re-read the documents, he felt convinced that the King had delayed sending them in order that they might arrive on the very eve of the meeting of the Commission so that "I might be overwhelmed with them on the sudden and have no time to deliberate, before we were to come the second time to sit in judgement".[2] He spent another sleepless night, turning over in his mind the probable consequences of his firmness against the King—"how Papists would scorn at it, how it might be my own ruin . . . a hazard to my friends, and the

---

[1] The text is given in W. Cobbett, op. cit., II, pp. 860 ff; Sloane MSS. (British Museum), 3828, ff. 1–2.

[2] *Account*, p. 820.

Commissioners which were of my mind". But he was determined to abide by his conscience, which "was more to me than all the world; that it was a fearful thing, in place of judgement, to give a sentence against my own heart".[1] Having thus strengthened his resolution, he slept. Next morning "I found my heart much settled in that which I held to be the truth". First, he prayed earnestly to God, "remembering . . . that he had from time to time rid me out of all my troubles". Then he read the King's letter again and thought that he could detect the hand of Rochester behind it. After that he drove up from Croydon to Lambeth, where he met with the news of the death of Sir Thomas Overbury, although he had neither the time nor the knowledge to trace the fateful connection between that death and the present divorce case. He was much more concerned with the immediate proceedings and the Bishop of London told him that the eyes of the whole Church of England were upon him and that he "should show" himself "a worthy man".

The proceedings of the Commission were short, for Abbot carried a motion unanimously that the Earl of Essex should be recalled for further examination. After the Court rose, Abbot asked the Bishop of Lichfield and Coventry to inform the King of what had occurred. Then he returned to Croydon. The next day was Sunday and he preached on the raising of the widow's son at Nain, "to the great comfort of my soul".[2] On Monday the Commissioners dealt quietly with minor matters, but afterwards the Bishop of Lichfield told Abbot that the King would not permit the recall of Essex, lest "he might speak somewhat which might mar the business". To such lengths was James prepared to go to secure the divorce. For Abbot it marked the end of any hope of a just issue to the proceedings. "If that be denied", he said, "and we have no further proof, I shall never give sentence for the nullity. As good declare my mind at first as at last, and I pray you so acquaint His Majesty."

The next session of the Commission was on Wednesday. Before the proceedings began Sir Thomas Lake waited on the Commissioners with a message from the King desiring a speedy end of the business and ordering them to pronounce sentence on Saturday. For three more days the Commissioners argued. On

[1] Ibid.　　　　[2] Ibid., p. 822.

Thursday, when that day's meeting was ended, an attempt was made by those Commissioners who were willing to vote in favour of the divorce to convince Abbot and his supporters, but to no avail. On Friday morning Abbot went to Whitehall to make a final attempt to induce the King to see reason. James took him on one side to the window of the royal gallery and asked him how the case was proceeding. Once more they went over the old ground, Abbot being much troubled and with tears in his eyes during most of the interview. He made it quite clear to the King that "I would not give sentence where I saw no proof",[1] and he was outspoken in his condemnation of the King's attitude, telling him that "he must never afterwards expect true service of me, for how could I be true to him, who was false under God?" When the interview was over the King, much moved by Abbot's sad earnestness, walked away to report the conversation to the Earl of Suffolk.

Abbot returned to Lambeth for dinner and had an interview with the Bishop of Bath and Wells (James Montague), who gave him "no discouragement". Then he received an unexpected visit from the Bishop of Lichfield, who this time brought from the King "a treatise upon the present argument", written by a Scotsman. Abbot read it in his coach on the way to Croydon and thought it feeble.[2] He had decided to withdraw from Lambeth in order to avoid further distractions and after his arrival at Croydon he attended to domestic business, prayed, and went to bed. Rising very early he went to his study and made notes for a speech he intended to deliver when sentence was pronounced. Then he drove up to Lambeth and worked again on the speech, which was a masterly apologia of his own position and a damaging exposure of the Countess's case. In it[3] he stated that he was concerned that "before the separation be pronounced, it must appear unto the Church that there is good cause for the same",

[1] Ibid., p. 825.

[2] "This treatise no way pleased me; but I thought it the work of some hungry fellow, who lacked 20/- to buy food to his belly"—ibid., p. 826.

[3] "The SPEECH intended to be spoken at Lambeth, Sept. 25 1613, by George, Archbishop of Canterbury, when it came to his turn to declare his mind concerning the Nullity of Marriage between the Earl of Essex and Lady Frances Howard"—Sloane MSS. (British Museum), 3828, f 35 ff, printed in W. Cobbett, op cit., II, 844 ff.

and this "good cause" must be based, not on surmises or sugges-tions, but on proofs, "which may give full contentment to the conscience of the judge". He listed his doubts in the present case, of which the following are the most important:

1. The uncertainty of the proceedings. First the plea had been *frigidatus versus hanc*; then it had been *maleficiatus versus hanc*; then *maleficiatus* had been dropped and doubts had been raised as to whether such a plea was a lawful ground for a nullity. "I think of this case of my lord's which is built on such a foundation as no man will stand to. . . . We are on it, and off it, and avow it we dare not, yet fly it we will not. . . . How should I assent to that whereof I can learn no certainty from the Counsel of my lady, nor from you that be the judges, who speak for this nullity."

2. The novelty of the plea. There was no precedent of "a person whose marriage was annulled for impotency towards his wife, when he found an ability of carnal copulation with any other woman". It is "a thing unheard of in our church, and unknown in our kingdom".

3. The insufficiency of proof. "I find nothing [in all the deposi-tions] which is not in substance contained in the Answer of my lord of Essex", and Essex had alleged no impotency but had stated only that he had never carnally known the Countess and that the fault in this lay with her. No other proofs had been forthcoming.

4. The manner in which the sentence was to be given. It was to be given in general terms, without stating reasons. "Let us have, I pray you, some kind of satisfaction, and let not this enigma in general blind us, lest the world would say, that wilfully we shut our eyes against the truth."

5. The inconvenience which will follow if the marriage is annulled. "Whatever couple . . . who have no children, and live discontented, come presently to take part of this general jubilee."

When he had finished working on this speech, Abbot saw in turn the Bishop of London, Sir John Bennett, Dr James, and Dr Edwards, and each expressed his agreement with Abbot's conviction that there were no grounds for pronouncing a nullity. The Archbishop then planned his campaign. He arranged that

Dr James and Dr Edwards should speak first and outline briefly the objections to pronouncing a nullity, and then Sir John Bennett should give an extended judgement. Afterwards Abbot would call on the other Commissioners to speak while the Bishop of London took notes. The Bishop of London would answer the points made by the other side, and finally Abbot himself would make his prepared speech. "Leave it to me," he said, "and I doubt not, in Almighty God, but to batter this nullity to dust."[1] Abbot's confidence was well-founded, for the speech he had prepared was damaging to the whole case, and even if the divorce still went through, he would have declared to the world the flimsy nature of the evidence upon which judgement had been pronounced.

But the speech was destined never to be delivered. Once again Abbot had made a fatal mistake, for during his interview with the King the previous day he had told James that "when I am in the place of judgement, I would not conceal the reason of my sentence".[2] The King being thus warned took immediate steps to silence the Commissioners. While they were awaiting the late arrival of the Bishop of Winchester, Sir Thomas Lake appeared bearing a message from the King which he had been instructed to deliver when all the Commissioners were together. There was a further delay and then the Bishop of Winchester arrived and Sir Thomas was able to give the royal message. It ordered the Commissioners to deliver a simple verdict of Yea or Nay, and forbade them to give any reasons in open Court. Recognizing the impossibility of the situation, Abbot and his supporters withdrew, leaving Bishop Bilson of Winchester to pronounce the divorce, the six remaining Commissioners concurring.

Posterity must acknowledge the courageous and conscientious consistency of Abbot throughout these proceedings. He had been utterly convinced that there was insufficient proof to sustain the libel, that the plea itself was doubtful, and that the proceedings were inconsistent. From that position of conscience nothing had been able to move him, neither the persuasion and sharpness of the King, nor the slanders of the Howards, nor the intrigues and arguments of his opponents on the Commission. Throughout the country the sentence was condemned. For the first and only

---

[1] *Account*, p. 827.   [2] Ibid., p. 826.

time Abbot found himself a popular hero and letters of congratulation reached him from all parts.

> The Country was delighted to find that in that corrupt Court there was at least one who could hold his ground in opposition to the King's wishes, when a matter of conscience was at stake. . . . It was, as it were, the Spirit of Calvinism which had taken up its abode in that silent monitor; the one power in England which could resist the seductions of the Court, and which was capable of rebuking, at any cost, the immorality of the great.[1]

But the consequences of his stand were grave to him personally. This soon became evident, for shortly after the divorce suit was ended Bishop Neile was promoted to the See of Lincoln as a reward for his compliance and assistance, the King thus ignoring his former promise that the Archbishop's brother should receive the appointment. Never again did Abbot enjoy the full confidence of the King and from this point there begins the slow drift of this already isolated Primate into the political and ecclesiastical wilderness.

Although the Divorce Commission had completed its work, this was by no means the last that Abbot was to hear of the case, for the Howards resorted to every device in order to trick or trap the Archbishop into some admission that he had been mistaken and had withdrawn his opposition.[2] First, the rumour was circulated that Abbot and the Commissioners who had supported him, "after more mature deliberation, had testified their concurrence with the rest of the Commissioners, and all were now of one mind".[3] Then there was an attempt to bolster up the validity of the divorce by getting it certified under the Great Seal and, as part of this process, every effort was made to get Abbot to sign

---

[1] S. R. Gardiner, *History of England, 1603–42* (1883–4), II, pp. 174, 211.

[2] For the events that follow, see "Some observable Things, since 25 Sept., 1613, when the Sentence was given in the Cause of the Earl of Essex, continued unto the day of the Marriage, Dec. 26. 1613"—Sloane MSS. (British Museum), 3828, f. 23 ff, printed in W. Cobbett, op. cit., II, pp. 829 ff. In the following pages it will be referred to as *Observable Things*.

[3] *Observable Things*, p. 834.

the writ recording the sentence and thus to make it appear that he had consented to the proceedings. Finally, the Bishop of Lichfield and Coventry, acting on behalf of the Howards, called on Abbot a fortnight or so before the marriage of Lady Frances Howard to Rochester, who had now been created Earl of Somerset, was due to take place and attempted to persuade him to grant a licence for the marriage. Had the Archbishop complied with this request the Howards would have regarded it as tantamount to an approval of the whole proceedings. Abbot was able to avoid the trap by declining to issue the licence on the wholly proper ground that the Chapel Royal, where the marriage was to take place, was outside his jurisdiction and that for him to issue a licence, therefore, would be to usurp the prerogative of the Bishop of Bath and Wells, who, as Dean of the Chapel Royal, was the appropriate authority to grant a licence for the purpose. Abbot was quite awake to the Howard stratagem and he told the Bishop of Lichfield and Coventry,

> Many times . . . I have had it reiterated, that such a trick should be put upon me: that although it needed not, yet I should be moved for granting this licence, because thereby I should be constrained, either to grant it and so cross my former sentence and involvedly give my consent to the nullity, or I should deny it, and so grate once more again upon the King's displeasure.[1]

How did Abbot fare under "the King's displeasure"? Two days after the visit of the Bishop of Lichfield and Coventry, when the King had left London for Hampton Court, the Bishop of Bath and Wells called on Abbot at Lambeth and told him that he had a message from the King. His Majesty was surprised that the Archbishop had not spoken to him about the divorce sentence, and he expected him to make satisfaction and submission. Dr Montague believed that the King had "some scruple in his mind, which he wished should be removed before his going to the Communion on Christmas Day".[2] Consequently, when the King returned to Whitehall later in the week, Abbot went to the Court, "where they were all busy about plate and jewels against the marriage".[3] He

[1] *Observable Things*, p. 841.   [2] Ibid., p. 842.
[3] Ibid., p. 843.

72

had a conversation with the King, during which he said of the divorce: "I can say nothing more than this, that I was put into the Commission as a judge, and at the time of sentence I did my conscience; and since I have not meddled with the matter." The King questioned the accuracy of the last remark by bringing up Abbot's refusal to grant a marriage licence. Abbot replied that he had not refused, but that he had made it clear that the Bishop of Bath and Wells alone had authority to grant such a licence.

Abbot remained at Court for another half-hour and then returned home. That night a friend visited him and told him that he had heard from Lord Knollys that the Bishop of Lichfield and Coventry, Dr Neile, had seriously wronged him [i.e. Abbot], "for he had reported all the speech about the licence in a spiteful manner".[1] This news confirmed the suspicions Abbot already had that Neile had been responsible for many of his misfortunes, and he resolved "afterwards to be very wary how he trusted him". On Christmas Day the Archbishop attended on the King and received Communion with him, and on the following day he was present in the Chapel Royal for the marriage of Lady Frances and the Earl of Somerset. One may regret that he did not maintain his aloofness from the whole proceedings by staying away, but at least he did not officiate, and no doubt, realizing that his attitude was now well known, desired to end the affair. Perhaps his very presence bore witness to his disapproval. S. R. Gardiner commented: "Abbot was not a large-minded man, but on that day he stood in a position which placed him far above all the genius and the grandeur around him."[2] The Service over, he "had a pair of wedding-gloves, and so came home to dinner; where he sat with much comfort, as being glad, that since things must be so, they were come to an end".[3]

[1] Ibid., p. 844.   [2] Op. cit., II, p. 211.   [3] *Observable Things*, p. 844.

6

"The Insolences of Papists at Home and Abroad"

Of Papists there are three kinds. The "open Papist" which dwelleth among us and foresaketh our communion . . . protesting that we are departed from the Catholic Church and therefore that they may not in conscience join with us. The second sort are "fleeing Papists" which fleeing over the seas . . . return to steal away the hearts of subjects from the Prince. . . . The third the "cunning Papist" which can hide himself under the colour of loyalty and obedience to the laws, and will needs be accounted a faithful, true and good subject, and yet carrieth in his bosom the same persuasion that the other do, and for fear of danger or discredit, they are contented to obey the law.

A contemporary preacher, quoted in W. P. M. Kennedy,
Parish Life under Queen Elizabeth

ARCHBISHOP ABBOT was among those who on 5 April 1614, a dull and stormy Tuesday, attended James I when he went to Westminster in solemn procession and with great pomp to open the second Parliament of his reign. In common with all the Stuarts, James suffered from a chronic shortage of money and from an inability to retrench. From this there sprang the perennial conflict between Crown and Parliament, for whenever the King appealed to Parliament for supplies, the Commons always countered with a demand for the redress of their grievances, among which was included the King's non-parliamentary expedients for raising money. Moreover, demands for money were inextricably confused in the popular mind with the emergency of war. It was considered that a crisis alone justified a demand for money, and consequently, when there was no such crisis, Parliament persistently refused to help the Government to finance its daily responsibilities. The first Parliament of the reign had broken up on this issue in 1610 and the conception of the Great Contract came to nothing. In 1612, however, the royal

74

debt had amounted to £500,000 with an annual deficit of £160,000. All suggested projects for increasing revenue were inadequate and "it was this grinding pressure of financial necessity that finally forced James to summon the Addled Parliament".[1]

In the Lords the Crown held the dominant position, but in the Commons the situation was reversed. A large proportion of Privy Councillors sat in the Upper House, whereas there were only three or four in the Lower House. Moreover, the Lords included the Howard faction, which supported the Crown. "When the Addled Parliament met, the Howard–Somerset alliance was firmly cemented. Despite the opposition of Abbot, Ellesmere, and Pembroke, the Spanish faction, astutely promoted by Sarmiento, the Spanish Ambassador, gained a complete ascendancy at Court."[2]

Abbot was most assiduous in his attendance at this Parliament and was present at every sitting. After an inauspicious speech from the King the Houses separated and once again difficulties and tensions became apparent. It was clear that the Commons had no intention of granting supplies to the King before their grievances were dealt with and they requested the Lords for a conference on impositions. The Lords delayed their reply while they debated the question. Lord Chancellor Ellesmere proposed that before they answered the Commons they should request the judges to pronounce on the legality of impositions. Abbot was among those who supported this suggestion,[3] and the motion was carried; but when the judges reported that they felt unable to deliver an opinion before the case had been argued, the Lords, on Tuesday 24 May, returned to the original request of the Commons. Abbot was among the Privy Councillors who as a body opposed a meeting with the Commons. He addressed the House to that effect, and in the end the Lords decided not to have such a meeting.

While these debates were in progress, the Bishop of Lincoln, Richard Neile, had made bitter attacks upon the Commons, accusing them of sedition and describing the subject of impositions as a *noli me tangere*. This angered the Commons to such a degree that they refused to transact further business until they had received satisfaction for this insult. For the first time the Privy Councillors in the Lords split over this issue and Abbot was

[1] Thomas L. Moir, *The Addled Parliament of 1614* (1958), pp. 10 f.
[2] Ibid., p. 65.   [3] Ibid., p. 118.

among the group which demanded an explanation from Neile. In adopting this line he was, characteristically, opposing the Howard group which objected to an oral accusation from the Commons based only on rumour. After some wrangling between the two Houses and a heated debate in the Commons, the King informed the Commons on 3 June that unless they voted supply he would dissolve Parliament. When the Commons held their ground James, advised by Northampton and assured by the Spanish Ambassador that the King of Spain would see him through financially, dissolved Parliament on 7 June.

Obviously this abortive Parliament had done nothing to relieve the King's financial straits, and in order that he might receive some assistance Abbot and the bishops decided to offer him a gift in the form of plate. Writing to the Bishop of London, Abbot spoke of the fiasco of the late Parliament as "an event producing a great damp on all sides", and he said that the bishops had resolved that each of them "should voluntarily send unto the King the best piece of plate which he had", and that if the King would accept the gift they had promised to move "the civilians and others of the abler sort of the clergy . . . to do the same".[1] Abbot himself led the way with a gift of a bason and ewer, which were redeemed for £140,[2] and the example thus set by the bishops was followed by the rest of the Council and by many of the nobles.

The dissolution marked the triumph of the Howard party, but their position was by no means impregnable. Earlier that year Abbot had struck a sharp blow at Northampton's position. The latter was Warden of the Cinque Ports, an office which he used to help smuggle Roman priests and spies in and out of the country. "As some counter to this the Archbishop had a standing arrangement with the landlord of the King's Head at Canterbury that the pockets and luggage of suspicious-looking travellers should be gone through carefully whenever possible and any incriminating matter brought to light."[3] In the spring of 1614 Northampton was openly accused of "having told Bellarmine that his writings

---

[1] Archbishop of Canterbury to the Bishop of London, June 1614—J.R. Tanner, *Constitutional Documents of the Reign of James I* (1930), p. 362.

[2] Chamberlain to Carleton, 30 June 1614—McClure, I, p. 542.

[3] W. McElwee, *The Murder of Sir Thomas Overbury* (1952), p. 154.

against the Church of Rome were only a necessary piece of camouflage to delude King James".[1] Shortly afterwards he retired in disgrace to his country house, "and it was said that Abbot had actually been able to produce some treasonable correspondence with Bellarmine, secured for him by his innkeeper friend, in which Northampton had confessed that 'his heart stood with the Papists'".[2]

Abbot was now to play a leading part in another counter-stroke against the Howards. During the summer term James I paid a visit to Cambridge University, where a young man named George Villiers performed a minor part in one of the undergraduate plays. He had been selected by the anti-Howard party as a potential candidate for the royal favour, and if the plan succeeded it would mean that the current favourite, the Earl of Somerset, would have been supplanted by one of their own party. Abbot was a man whose motives were always serious, and there can be no doubt that he regarded Somerset as a menace to the country. Somerset had been dazzled by Spain and he was dangerous to the Protestant cause at home and abroad. In addition, it had been because of him that Abbot had had to pass through the turmoil of the Essex Divorce. The effect which Villiers's appearance had on the King at Cambridge was watched carefully and reported to Abbot. The Archbishop, encouraged by what he heard and by the news of another meeting between the King and Villiers in Northumberland, induced the Earl of Pembroke and Sir Thomas Lake to join him in the plan to substitute Villiers in place of Somerset in the King's affections. A meeting of the anti-Howard faction was held at Baynard's Castle, as a result of which it was decided to procure for Villiers a post in the Royal Bedchamber. For the present, however, little progress was made, apart from the effect of the King's new interest on Somerset, who acted impetuously and unwisely in face of his danger, so that James experienced a gradual disillusionment regarding him.

On 6 August an attempt was made on the Archbishop's life. He was sitting in his study dictating a letter to his secretary when a man rushed in with a knife. The man afterwards maintained that he had intended merely to tear Abbot's rochet, but the Archbishop was on him before he could do any damage to life or dress,

[1] Ibid. [2] Ibid.

while the intruder launched into a tirade of abuse, "with a countenance as wicked as the devil's". The Archbishop's servants soon overpowered him and put him in the stocks. The man stated that he was a Papist who "detested our religion as he did the devil", and thus led the Archbishop to surmise that "he was sent in by some Jesuitical persons who knew the house, for he avoided the great chamber where were at least half a score persons". After examining the man, Abbot committed him to prison.[1] Before the month of August was out Abbot was delivered from a danger of a somewhat different kind. He was eating a meal at the end of a fast day when a fish-bone became lodged in his throat. His condition was regarded as serious and it was several days before he "escaped" this "shrewd danger".[2]

In April 1615 Abbot and his party made a move to further the fortunes of Villiers. James had received many recriminations and reproaches from the Queen for the influence which he had allowed Somerset to have with him, and he was determined that if he was going to admit Villiers into closer intimacy he would do so only if he was asked to do so by the Queen. Abbot later narrated[3] how he and other lords begged the Queen to recommend to the King that Villiers be made a Gentleman of the Bedchamber. "My Lord," the Queen replied, "you and your friends know not what you ask. I know your master better than you all, for if this young man be once brought in, the first persons he will plague will be you that labour for him." Abbot, however, successfully won the Queen round and on 2 August, in a somewhat dramatic manner, she asked James to knight Villiers and to make him a Gentleman of the Bedchamber. Somerset was in the ante-chamber and overheard the conversation. He sent in a message that Villiers should only be a groom of the bedchamber, but Abbot, who was also close at

[1] Abbot to William Trumbull, 31 Aug. 1614—Downshire MSS. (*Hist. MSS. Comm. Reports,* Series 75 (5), p. 511). Four years later another attempt was made on Abbot's life by Edward Worsly who was committed to the Tower and then to the Marshalsea. Abbot mediated, however, and he was set at liberty, but banished from the country—"A Warrant to the Keeper of the Marshalsea, 26th July 1618" (*Acts of the Privy Council of England,* xxxv, p. 231).

[2] John Sanford to William Trumbull, 23 Aug. 1614—Downshire MSS. (*Hist. MSS. Comm. Reports,* Series 75 (5), p. 502).

[3] "Archbishop Abbot his Narrative", in J. Rushworth, *Historical Collections of private passages of state, etc.* (1659), I, pp. 434 ff.

hand, sent in a counter-message to the Queen requesting her to insist that he should receive the higher office. In this Abbot was successful and thus won a decisive victory over the anti-Howard party. But so far as he personally was concerned it was a Pyrrhic victory and he later acknowledged that the Queen's original objection had been prophetic. Those who promoted Villiers, particularly Abbot, received no lasting gratitude from him. Abbot told how, at the beginning of his career, Villiers had asked him to "give him some lessons how he should carry himself". Abbot commended to him three principles of conduct. "The first was, That daily upon his knees he should pray to God to bless the King his master, and to give him [George] grace, studiously to serve and please him. The second was, That he should do all good offices between the King and the Queen, and between the King and the Prince. The third was, That he should fill his Majesty's ears with nothing but the truth."[1] He made Villiers repeat these maxims to him, requested him to tell the King of them, and then to report to him what the King said. The next day Abbot was in the Gallery at Whitehall with the Prince's tutor when Villiers approached and told the tutor "how much he was beholden" to Abbot. He had told the King about the Archbishop's three principles and James had said that "they were instructions worthy of an archbishop to give to a young man".[2] The relationship which existed in these early days between the Archbishop and Villiers is revealed in a letter which Abbot wrote to "my George" in December after the fall of Somerset had left the way clear for Villiers. He declared that: "I will from this day forward respect and esteem you for my son, and so hereafter know yourself to be." This was followed by some sober advice about serving the King diligently and being wary of suitors, and was signed, "Your very loving father, G. CANT".[3] In these early days Villiers possessed a courtesy, a hesitation and an uncertainty which made him pleasing to those around him, but in time these gave way to arrogance, obstinacy, and ingratitude. Thus Abbot later commented that Villiers's gratitude to him continued for a time, "but not long, either to me, or other of his well-wishers".[4]

[1] "Archbishop Abbot his Narrative".   [2] Ibid.
[3] Abbot to Sir George Villiers, 10 Dec. 1615—G. Goodman, *The Court of King James I* (ed. J. S. Brewer, 1839), II, pp. 160 f.   [4] Ibid.

The time was to come when Abbot would lay all his misfortunes at the door of Villiers. But the wider results of Abbot's initiative in introducing Villiers to the King were far more important than his personal misfortunes. It had fatal consequences for Church and State, and S. L. Lee rightly described it as "the most disastrous step Abbot ever took".[1]

After the dissolution of the Addled Parliament, the King in his penury, acting on the advice of the Howards and under the influence of the Spanish Ambassador, was most anxious to make an alliance with Spain. He accordingly reopened negotiations for a Spanish marriage for the Prince of Wales, in the hope that if such a contract could be arranged the Spanish bride would bring with her a sufficient dowry to compensate for the Commons' lack of co-operation in granting supplies. It is unnecessary to describe the prolonged negotiations, but in May 1615 Spain sent certain Articles which were to serve as a basis for such negotiations. The crux of the matter was the condition made by Spain that a marriage was contingent upon the ultimate repeal of the anti-Papal laws in England.

Throughout the negotiations Abbot remained firm in his opposition. He was at this time busy seeking out and punishing all evidence of popery and enforcing the recusancy fines. He maintained a continuous correspondence with William Trumbull, the British envoy at Brussels, in which he inquired about many Papists or suspected Papists in the Spanish Netherlands who had contact with England, had escaped from these shores, or were expected to cross to England.[2] Among the State Papers there are numerous letters from Abbot about the apprehension, examination, and punishment of Papists.[3] In 1612 he had taken considerable interest in the conversion of two Carmelite Friars. Sir Dudley Carleton had asked John Chamberlain to introduce these two to the Archbishop,[4] and when they arrived in June one was lodged with Abbot and the other was to go to the Archbishop of York.[5] They made a public confession of their faith and of their

---

[1] *D.N.B.*, "Abbot, George".
[2] Cf. Downshire MSS.—*Hist. MSS. Comm. Reports*, Series 75 (4), *passim*.
[3] Cf., e.g., *S.P. Dom. Jas. I*, lxxx, 113; lxxxi, 54, 59, 66; lxxxii, 99, 111.
[4] Carleton to Chamberlain, 29 April 1612—*S.P. Dom. Jas. I*, lxviii, 103.
[5] Chamberlain to Carleton, 17 June 1612—*S.P. Dom. Jas. I*, lxix, 71.

conversion to the Church of England, but two years later, "not being promoted as they hoped",[1] they had forsworn their new allegiance and had petitioned to return to Rome. Abbot committed them to safe custody,[2] and a month later he sent Sir Dudley Carleton a full account of the case, in which he alleged that "they were tampered with" by the chaplain to the Venetian Ambassador, and that the Spanish Ambassador had also meddled in the affair. He concluded by expressing the wish that "the insolences of Papists at home and abroad were punished".[3] It is abundantly clear that Abbot was in no mood to give any sort of support to a Spanish marriage.

Throughout the summer of 1615 the Archbishop was unwell. "He hath been very crazy all this summer," wrote Chamberlain, "and for all his good order and diet is thought to have but an unsound body."[4] For a fortnight in July he was ill with ague,[5] but on 19 July he was about again and at the Council table.[6] A few days later he went in state to spend the rest of the summer at Canterbury.[7] This was his first visit to his cathedral city since his election four years ago.[8] Back in London he found that rumours were circulating about the calling of a new Parliament. The King's financial position was worse than ever and negotiations with Spain were certain to be protracted; but although a Parliament appeared to be the only solution, the pro-Spanish party were opposed to such a course because they feared that the Commons would denounce the King's Spanish policy. Towards the end of September the Council spent several days discussing the question and Abbot was among those who were wholly in favour of summoning a new Parliament. He was the last speaker and he said that he agreed with those who held that the King's financial relief "could no way so honourable be done as by the good will

---

[1] Abbot to the Bishop of Bath and Wells, Jan. 1614—*S.P. Dom. Jas. I,* lxvi, 9. i.

[2] Chamberlain to Carleton, 3 Feb. 1614—*S.P. Dom. Jas. I,* lxxvi, 18.

[3] Abbot to Carleton, 16 March 1614—*S.P. Dom. Jas. I,* lxxvi, 48.

[4] Chamberlain to Carleton, 24 Aug. 1615—McClure, I, p. 612.

[5] Same to same, 13 July 1615—McClure, I, p. 606.

[6] Same to same, 20 July 1615—McClure, I, p. 610.

[7] Same to same, 24 Aug. 1615—McClure, I, p. 612.

[8] Revd Thomas Horne to Carleton, 7 Aug. 1615—*S.P. Dom. Jas. I,* lxxxi, 46.

of his Majesty's people in Parliament". At the same time he was not averse to such electioneering devices as would secure a Parliament "so prepared and ordered, as might carry with it a liklihood and probability of bringing good success".[1] When the meeting was over the King asked what had been done and Abbot, who "had taken large notes of what had passed",[2] made a summary report to his Majesty. In the event Parliament was not summoned for another six years.

Up in Scotland the Scottish bishops had excommunicated the Marquis of Huntley for suspected popery and intrigue. Although the Marquis made no effort to change his ways the King permitted him to come to Court, and when he expressed a wish to communicate in the Church of England James sent him to Abbot to see if he could be absolved for his excommunication. It was contrary to Canon Law "that one excommunicated by the Church should, without their consent who had so sentenced him, be absolved by another".[3] This difficulty was overcome by obtaining the consent of the Bishop of Caithness, in the name of the clergy of Scotland, and on 7 July 1616, in the chapel of Lambeth Palace, Abbot absolved the Marquis. The Church of Scotland took exception to these proceedings, regarding it as a slight upon their independence, and Abbot wrote to Archbishop Spottiswoode to explain his action, which he defended on three grounds. First, he freely acknowledged the independence of the Church of Scotland, but what he had done was performed in a spirit of "brotherly correspondence and unity of affection". Secondly, it was permitted for the Church of England to receive to its communion a person excommunicated, "if the said person did declare he had a purpose hereafter for some time to reside, which the lord marquis did openly profess that he intended". Thirdly, he had the Bishop of Caithness's assurance that the Church of Scotland would not think ill of the action.[4] The letter satisfied the offended clergy, but it was resolved that the absolution would not be effective when the

---

[1] "Discussion in Council on the Question of calling a new Parliament, 28th Sept. 1615" in *The Letters and Life of Francis Bacon* (ed. J. Spedding, 1861-74), V, p. 205.

[2] Ibid.

[3] John Spottiswoode, *History of the Church of Scotland* (1851), III, p. 231.

[4] Abbot to Spottiswoode, 23 July 1616—Spottiswoode, op. cit., p. 232.

Marquis returned to Scotland.[1] It is not easy to understand Abbot's motives in thus absolving one suspected of popery, for it is not what would have been expected from one who was such an anti-Papist. It is true that the King was anxious that it should be done and that the doing of it should not be delayed,[2] but Abbot was most unlikely to be moved by that if he saw good reason why it should not be done.

During this year (1616) Abbot once again showed his concern over the indiscipline of the members of All Souls, Oxford. "I require you, Mr Warden, and the rest of the officers", he wrote, "to punish such of your Society as, neglecting their studies, do spend their time abroad in taverns and alehouses to the defamation of scholars and scandal of your House."[3] The following year he warned the college to be peaceable in the election of its officers,[4] and when he learnt that seven members of the college had made "a rupture concerning the proctorship" he ordered them to confess their fault in the chapel before the Warden and Fellows.[5] The Warden of the college, Richard Mocket, who had been Abbot's chaplain, put the Archbishop in an embarrassing position by the publication of a book entitled, *De Polita Ecclesiae Anglicanae,* in which he skilfully selected quotations from the Homilies in order to convey a Calvinist impression. What was more important was that "he ascribed to the Archbishop of Canterbury a higher position in the government than the government found convenient or that the event proved to be true".[6] Abbot's support of Mocket failed to prevent the condemnation and public burning of the book, and the Archbishop was much affected by this, being "off the hooks" for some time afterwards.[7]

Meanwhile the Spanish marriage negotiations pursued their frustrating and tedious way. In an attempt to prod Spain into greater activity Sir Walter Raleigh was released from prison and permitted to make a voyage in search of gold in Guiana, a project

[1] Spottiswoode, ibid.　　　　[2] Ibid., p. 231.
[3] Abbot to the College, 21 Nov. 1616—C. T. Martin, *Catalogue of the Archives of All Souls* (1877), p. 312; M. Burrows, *Worthies of All Souls* (1874), p. 126.
[4] Abbot to the College, 26 April 1617—C. T. Martin, op. cit., p. 312.
[5] Abbot to the College, 22 May 1617—ibid.
[6] Hugh Trevor-Roper, *Archbishop Laud* (1940), p. 50.
[7] P. Heylyn, *Cyprianus Anglicus* (1668), p. 75.

which might lead to collision with the Spaniards in the area. Spain, alarmed at this sign of English aggressiveness, hastened to give new life to the marriage negotiations and in April 1617 King James sent Sir John Digby to Spain to draw up a marriage treaty. The King discussed the negotiations with the Council, but the anti-Spanish faction, including Abbot, were excluded from the deliberations.[1] Back in January the Venetian Secretary had had a long conversation with Abbot, during which the latter had declared that he was "not greatly inclined to the Spaniards. . . . The marriage with Spain shall not be made, and the Spaniards shall never set their feet in this island."[2] It would appear, however, that he had not as yet offered extreme opposition to the negotiations nor to the dispatch of Digby, "reserving himself so to do with the rest of the clergy when they come to the point of religion, upon which and the manner of bringing up the children and some other questions, there may arise such difficulties that the whole affair may end in nothing yet".[3] Abbot displayed considerable foresight in thus expressing his opinion that the marriage would flounder of its own accord.

Abbot was deeply grieved at the death of his brother Robert, Bishop of Salisbury, in March 1618,[4] in spite of the fact that Robert had caused him much displeasure a few years earlier when at the age of sixty he had made a second marriage. His brother regarded this as an infringement of the apostolic injunction that a bishop should be the husband of one wife,[5] and—according to Peter Heylyn—he had written to Robert "such a sharp and bitter letter, so full of Reproaches and Revilings, that not being able to bear the burden of so great an insolency, he presently took thought upon it, and as presently died".[6]

As a protest against the sabbatarianism of the Puritans, who attempted to prohibit sports and games on Sunday, the King published in May 1618 the *Declaration of Sports,* commending

[1] Venetian Secretary to the Doge and Senate, 25 May 1617—*S.P. Venetian,* xiv, no. 771.

[2] Same to same, 19 Jan. 1617—ibid. no. 601.

[3] Same to same, 6 April 1617—ibid., no. 178.

[4] Sir Nathaniel Brent to Sir Dudley Carleton, 7 March 1618—*S.P. Dom. Jas. I,* xcvi, 7. Robert Abbot had been appointed to the see in 1615.

[5] 1 Tim. 3. 2.

[6] P. Heylyn, *Cyprianus Anglicus* (1668), p. 75.

suitable games and pastimes for Sunday.[1] When he ordered the declaration to be read by the clergy from their pulpits, Abbot was foremost in the opposition, for the sanctioning of such amusements seemed to him to imperil the faith of the people. On the day when the declaration was due to be read he was at Croydon and he forbade it to be read in the parish church there, "which the King was pleased to wink at, notwithstanding the daily endeavours that were used to irritate the King against him".[2] In the end James withdrew his command that the declaration should be publicly read, but the incident cannot have endeared the Archbishop to him.

During 1618 Abbot sent Sir Nathaniel Brent on a highly secret mission to Venice to obtain a copy of the *History of the Council of Trent,* which was being written by Padre Paulo and Padre Fulgentio. Brent sent it over to England in parts as it was written and then returned to translate it.[3] The same year Abbot was one of the judges in Star Chamber in the proceedings against a man named Wraynham who had been accused of slandering Lord Chancellor Bacon for injustice. He was sentenced to imprisonment and a heavy fine, and Abbot agreed with the sentence in a lengthy speech in which he appealed to numerous Scriptural precedents for the impartiality which should be found in judges. "Therefore," he concluded,

> since Wraynham hath blasphemed, spoken evil, and slandered a chief magistrate as any in the kingdom, it remaineth that in honour to God, and in duty and justice to the King and kingdom, that he should receive severe punishment. . . . Wherefore, if greater punishment had been given him, I should have assented; for justice belongeth to us, but mercy to our gracious sovereign.[4]

On 2 March 1619 Abbot lost one of his most influential friends at Court, for on that day the Queen died. Queen Anne had always

[1] E. Cardwell, *Documentary Annals of the Reformed Church of England* (1839), II, pp. 188–93.

[2] J. Nichols, *The Progresses, processions, and magnificent festivities of King James the First . . .* (1828), III, p. 397.

[3] Letters from Abbot to Nathaniel Brent, July/Sept. 1618—L. Atterbury (ed.), *Some Letters relating to the History of the Council of Trent* (1705), pp. 6–11. Brent's translation was published in 1620.

[4] W. Cobbett, *Complete Collection of State Trials* (1809), II, pp. 1085 f.

looked favourably upon the Archbishop in spite of their differing religious opinions. The Queen's religious convictions had always been something of an enigma. Apparently she had become reconciled to the Church of Rome in 1600 or 1601 and had received Communion in that Church on several occasions before she came to England in 1603. She had refused to communicate according to the Anglican rite at her Coronation and does not appear to have ever received the Anglican sacrament. On the other hand, she regularly attended the Anglican services conducted by her almoner. On her death-bed she was earnestly moved by Abbot and the Bishops of London and Worcester "to prepare herself and set all things in order", but "she could not be persuaded that her end was so near".[1] Abbot and the two bishops made a last attempt to wean her from Romanism. "Madam," said the Archbishop, "we hope your majesty doth not trust in your own merits, nor to the mediation of saints, but only by the blood and merits of our Saviour Christ Jesus you shall be saved." According to a contemporary account, she replied: "I do, and withal I renounce the mediation of all saints, and my own merits, and do only rely upon my Saviour Christ, who has redeemed my soul with his blood."[2] On 13 May the funeral took place at Westminster. Abbot occupied a prominent place in the funeral procession, and at the service he preached the sermon on the text: "For when the breath of man goeth forth he shall turn again to his earth: and then all his thoughts perish."[3]

Shortly after this, the Earl of Suffolk, the Lord Treasurer, was accused of corruption and peculation. In October or November he was summoned before the Star Chamber and on the last day of the trial Abbot was among those who delivered judgement. "My Lord of Canterbury's discourse suitable to his profession was of the abuse of extorting officers who like ill shepherds did tear and not shear the sheep."[4] Deprived of office, imprisoned in

[1] Chamberlain to Carleton, 6 March 1619—McClure, II, p. 219.

[2] Letter dated 27 March 1619—*Miscellany of the Abbotsford Club* (1837), I, pp. 81 ff.

[3] Ps. 146. 3—"Description of the funeral procession, interment, etc. of Queen Anne . . . ", 13 May 1619 (*S.P. Dom. Jas. I,* Addenda, 13 May 1619). The sermon is not extant.

[4] Sir John Finet to the Earl of Salisbury, 14 Nov. 1619—Cecil MSS. 129, ff. 169–73, quoted D. Mathew, *The Jacobean Age* (1938), p. 330.

the Tower, ordered to pay a heavy fine, the downfall of Suffolk marked the final crumbling of the Howard faction.

Abbot always retained a great affection for his native town of Guildford and for some years he had been making arrangements for establishing a hospital in the town near to Holy Trinity Church. It was to consist of a Master, twelve brethren, and eight sisters, and Abbot endowed the foundation with land to the value of £300. On Tuesday 6 April 1619 he laid the foundation stone of the Hospital of the Blessed Trinity, and during succeeding years he watched carefully over its progress. Attached to it were a chapel and rooms for his own private use and thither he often retired for rest and seclusion.[1] At the end of the month Abbot was stricken with gout and was confined to his house for a week.[2]

A crisis had now occurred which threatened the pro-Spanish policy of James and his advisers. James's son-in-law, Frederick of the Palatinate, with youthful and innate innocence and optimism, had accepted the throne of Bohemia after the latter had revolted and deposed the Hapsburg Emperor Ferdinand. It was a foolish decision, taken against all advice, and its consequences were to unleash upon Europe the terrors of the Thirty Years War.[3] Spain was bound to the Emperor by ties of blood and interest and she joined with the Emperor and the Roman Catholic princes in Germany in a campaign to drive the Elector out of Bohemia. The Bohemians begged James for assistance, and a wave of anti-Papist and anti-Spanish sentiment swept across England while the King hesitated irresolutely and thus angered and dismayed the nation. On 12 September he addressed the Council on the subject. Abbot was ill with gout but from his sick-bed he addressed a letter to Secretary Naunton. He advised that there should be no hanging back, for "I am satisfied in my conjecture that the cause is just". It was God who had set up the Elector to propagate the Gospel and to protect the oppressed.

---

[1] Ernest G. R. Wale, *The Hospital of the Blessed Trinity, Guildford* (1933), p. 9. The Hospital was incorporated by royal charter in 1622 (*S.P. Dom. Jas. I,* cxxxi, 30—14 June 1622).

[2] Chamberlain to Carleton, 24 April 1619—McClure, II, p. 233.

[3] For the revolt in Bohemia and Frederick's acceptance of the throne, see C. V. Wedgwood, *The Thirty Years War* (1938), ch. 2.

He trusted that the Elector's cause would be seriously taken up, so "that it may appear to the world that we are awake when God in this sort calleth us". He suggested that on the matter of ways and means Parliament was the old and honourable way for supplying such needs.[1] This letter displayed a godly enthusiasm and a naïve crusading spirit, but it showed such utter lack of realism that it was evident that the writer had little grasp of the complexity of continental diplomacy. In any case, James was unwilling to endanger his negotiations with Spain by going to the assistance of Bohemia. Moreover, since the fall of the Howards, Villiers (now created Duke of Buckingham) was supreme and he was wholeheartedly in favour of the Spanish alliance. James was vexed with Frederick for what he regarded as an act of aggression against the Emperor, but, on the other hand, Frederick's wife was his daughter, his own flesh and blood, and the country was wholly in favour of measures to help the Elector. Torn this way and that, James vacillated and did nothing, while condemnation of his inaction continued to sweep the country. On 21 March 1620 Abbot told the King that his refusal to send help was sheer desertion of the cause of God,[2] and he begged the King to allow him to collect from the clergy a voluntary contribution for the relief of Frederick. Reluctantly, James granted permission on the condition that his own name was not mentioned. Thus on the same day the Archbishop and the Bishops of Durham and Winchester sent a circular letter to the bishops and clergy, urging "the more able" of them to lend money on behalf of Frederick and his wife, who "are unfortunate and in unsafe condition", and requesting them to send it as soon as possible. At the same time they instructed the clergy not "to preach of the war as one of religion, which would stir up all Europe".[3]

The Archbishop had proposed summoning a Parliament to provide ways and means for dealing with the situation in Bohemia. James still hesitated, but finally, when in August a Spanish army fell upon the Palatinate itself, he decided to summon Parliament, which met on 21 January. Abbot was absent from a number of

[1] Abbot to Naunton, 12 Sept. 1619—*Cabala. Mysteries of State, in Letters of the great Ministers of King James and King Charles* (1654), p. 169.
[2] S. R. Gardiner, *History of England, 1603–42* (1883–4), III, p. 339.
[3] *S.P. Dom. Jas. I*, cxiii, 34.

the sittings of this Parliament. On the first occasion (8 February), the Lord Treasurer excused his absence "by reason of Inconveniency of coming from his lordship's House, the Thames being frozen",[1] and later in the month he was absent "for Want of Health".[2] The Commons made the King a small and grossly inadequate grant towards war in Bohemia, but the King accepted it with delight, for after all it was money! Then the Commons turned to their grievances. In the Lords Lord Chancellor Bacon was condemned for bribery, but Abbot appears to have had little to do with it. He was on none of the three committees appointed by the House to examine witnesses, probably because of his absence for several days at the time when the matter was under discussion.[3] Sir Giles Mompesson was impeached in the Commons and Abbot was one of the Lords appointed to confer with the Commons on the question.[4] Sir Henry Yelverton was in trouble for insulting the King and the Duke of Buckingham, and when some of the Lords suggested that he should be censured without a hearing Abbot was among those who protested against the doctrine that an accused person should not be heard in his own defence.[5] For the rest, Abbot spoke on the question of dealing with Papists,[6] he sat on a number of Committees dealing with a great diversity of topics, he was appointed to open a discussion in a committee of Lords and Commons on the privileges of the Upper House,[7] and to him the Lords committed the task of admonishing in the Convocation House the Bishop of Llandaff (Theophilus Field) for "Brocage in Bribery".[8] There is no evidence that he displayed any qualities of leadership in the House, but he was a useful and able servant, fit to be called upon to act as chairman and spokesman.

After Easter relations between the King and the Commons

---

[1] *Journals of the House of Lords,* III, 8 Feb. 1621.

[2] Ibid., 15, 21, 23 Feb.

[3] *Journals of the House of Lords,* III, March–April.

[4] Ibid., 3 March.

[5] *Notes on Debates in the House of Lords, 1621* (ed. S. R. Gardiner, 1870), p. 78.

[6] *Notes on Debates in the House of Lords, 1621, 1625, 1628* (ed. F. H. Relf, 1929), p. 6.

[7] *Journals of the House of Lords,* III, 8 May.

[8] Ibid., 10 May.

became more strained, and, under pressure from Buckingham and the Spanish Ambassador, James adjourned Parliament early in June. Before it was recalled a blow had befallen the Archbishop which was to destroy any chance he might have had of leading opinion in the House of Lords or on the Council.

7

"A Man of Blood"?

Men in great place are thrice servants: servants of the sovereign or state; servants of fame; and servants of business. . . . The standing is slippery, and the regress is either a downfall, or at least an eclipse, which is a melancholy thing.

FRANCIS BACON, *Essay: Of Great Place*

I will wash my hands in innocency, O Lord: and so will I go to thine altar.

Psalm 26.6

NINE MILES south of Reading and to the east of the Reading-Alton road there stands high on a hill the fine Stuart mansion of Bramshill House, surrounded by a great and magnificent park. Lord Zouch bought the estate in 1605 and built the present house. Soon after it was completed Archbishop Abbot was invited to consecrate its chapel.[1] This was at the end of July 1621 and while he was there he joined a hunting and shooting expedition in the park. Apparently he had been advised by his doctor to hunt once a year in order to avoid the stone and the gout, to both of which he was subject.[2] The expedition ended in tragedy when the Archbishop shot an arrow from his cross-bow and killed Peter Hawkins, one of Lord Zouch's keepers. The circumstances of the accident are not altogether clear.[3] Lord Zouch himself asserted that the keeper "thrust himself behind a buck at which his grace was aiming".[4]

[1] Chamberlain to Carleton, 28 July 1621—*S.P. Dom. Jas. I*, cxxii, 46.

[2] "A Short Apology for Archbishop Abbot, touching the death of Peter Hawkins. By an Unknown hand", in *The English Works of Sir Henry Spelman* (ed. Edmund Gibson, 1727), pp. 105 ff.

[3] "No two of the authors cited relate the accident in the same way"— W. Cobbett, *Complete Collection of State Trials* (1809), II, p. 1162.

[4] Lord [Zouch] to Sir Edward Zouch, 24 July 1621—*S.P. Dom. Jas. I*, cxii, 37.

Sir Dudley Digges reported that the Archbishop shot at the deer "which, leaping up, the arrow struck the deerkeeper, who was hidden behind the herd".[1] Yet another version was retailed by the Venetian Ambassador, who reported that the Archbishop struck the keeper in the arm, "who was drunk and got in the way while riding on horseback".[2] Finally, John Hacket later described the accident as being due to the arrow glancing from a small bough and thus hitting the keeper.[3]

Whatever the precise circumstances of the affair, it is certain that the homicide was accidental, for the keeper had been warned more than once that day to keep out of the way and had ignored the warning.[4] At the same time there is some doubt about Abbot's skill with the cross-bow, for Sir Henry Spelman asserted that during the shoot the company had continually been told to stand very far off when the Archbishop shot, and later his discretion was questioned for "meddling with so dangerous an Engine in so great an Assembly".[5]

Two hundred years later Charles Kingsley, a descendant of Abbot's, who in the nineteenth century was rector of Eversley, the village beyond Bramshill, in one of his letters gave an imaginative reconstruction of the scene.

> I went out the other day to Bramshill park . . . And there I saw the very tree where an ancestor of mine, Archbishop Abbot, in James the First's time, shot the keeper by accident! I sat under the tree, and it all seemed to me like a present reality. I could fancy the old man . . . I could fancy the deer sweeping by, and the rattle of the cross-bow, and the white splinters sparkling off the fated tree as the bolt glanced and turned— and then the death shriek, and the stagger, and the heavy fall

[1] Sir Dudley Digges to Sir Dudley Carleton, 28 July 1621—*S.P. Dom. Jas. I*, cxxii, 47.

[2] Venetian Ambassador to the Doge and Senate, 13 Aug. 1621—*S.P. Venetian*, xvii, no. 130.

[3] John Hacket, *Scrinia Reserata, A Memorial offered to the great deservings of John Williams* (1692), p. 65.

[4] Sir Dudley Digges to Carleton, 28 July 1621—*S.P. Dom. Jas. I*, cxii, 47; "A Short Apology for Archbishop Abbot" in *The English Works of Sir Henry Spelman* (1727), pp. 105 ff.

[5] "An Answer to the Foregoing Apology", by Sir Henry Spelman, in *The English Works of Sir Henry Spelman*, p. 112.

of the sturdy forester—and the bow dropping from the old man's hands, and the blood sinking to his heart in one chilling rush, and his glorious features collapsing into that look of changeless and rigid sorrow, which haunted me in the portrait upon the wall in childhood.[1]

That is no doubt a highly coloured and subjective description, but it is evocative of that tragic incident and it conveys very vividly the devastating effect of the accident upon Abbot himself. Thomas Fuller said that it put an end not only "to the sport of that day", but also "almost to the Archbishop's mirth to the last of his life".[2] He at once made provision for the keeper's widow and for his children. The Venetian Ambassador stated that he gave £100 to each of the children and settled an annuity of £50 on the widow.[3] The latter figure was more probably £20, for that was the sum which Abbot in his will assured for her so long as she lived.[4]

The accident had legal ramifications, for having committed homicide Abbot had by Common Law forfeited his estates to the Crown and by Canon Law had committed an irregularity, the penalty for which was suspension from all ecclesiastical functions. The verdict of the Coroner's inquest was "death by misfortune and his own fault",[5] which, as John Chamberlain commented, "was a strange kind of verdict" and one which was contradictory in itself. When the Archbishop informed the King of what had happened, which he did immediately after the keeper died, James sent him a gracious answer "that such an accident might befall any man".[6] "The King says", wrote Sir Dudley Digges, "that none but a fool or a knave will think the worse of him for such

[1] F. E. Kingsley, *Charles Kingsley: His Letters and Memories of his Life* (1876), I, p. 76.

[2] T. Fuller, *Church History of Britain* (1655), Bk. x, sec. v, par. 12.

[3] Venetian Ambassador to the Doge and Senate, 13 Aug. 1621—*S.P. Venetian*, xvii, no. 130.

[4] "The Will of George Abbot", in *The Life of George Abbot, Lord Archbishop of Canterbury, reprinted with some Additions and Corrections from the* Biographia Britannica, *with his Character by the Right Hon. Arthur Onslow, Late Speaker of the House of Commons, Printed by John Russell* (1777), p. 66.

[5] "Per infortunium sua propria culpa"—Chamberlain to Carleton, 4 August 1621 (McClure, II, p. 395).

[6] Chamberlain to Carleton, 4 Aug. 1621—McClure, II, p. 395.

an accident, the like of which had once nearly happened to himself."[1] The King's unconcerned view was inevitably coloured by his own insatiable passion for the hunting field and he gladly excused the Archbishop from the Common Law penalties for his action.

The Archbishop was not to escape from the consequences of his misfortune quite so easily. "The fame of this man's death", wrote Fuller, "flew faster than the Arrow that killed him",[2] and very soon the opinion began to be expressed that, although it was not unheard of for bishops to hunt, it was unfortunate that an Archbishop of Canterbury should expose himself in this way to the possibility of committing homicide. "What should a man of his place and profession", Chamberlain wrote to Carleton, "be meddling with such edge-tools?"[3] It was the Canon Law aspect of the case, however, which brought the greatest trouble to the Archbishop.

The Lord Keeper, John Williams, had been appointed Bishop of Lincoln and was shortly to be consecrated to the episcopate, but he refused to accept consecration from an Archbishop whose hands were stained with blood. "For the king to leave *virum sanguineum,* a man of blood, Primate and Patriarch of all his Churches, is a thing that sounds very harsh in the old Courts and Canons of the Church."[4] Williams's objection was shared by William Laud,[5] whose consecration to the See of St David's was to take place at the same time. This unexpected scruple on the part of Williams was due less to conscience than to an innate ability to seize the main chance, for he undoubtedly regarded Abbot's irregularity (if that indeed could be proved) as a golden opportunity for securing the archbishopric for himself. He went so far as to remind Buckingham that "His Majesty hath promised me, upon my relinquishing the Great Seal, or before, one of the

---

[1] Sir Dudley Digges to Carleton, 28 July 1621—*S.P. Dom. Jas. I,* cxxii, 47.

[2] T. Fuller, op. cit., Bk. x, sec. v, par. 13.

[3] Chamberlain to Carleton, 4 Aug. 1621—McClure, II, p. 395.

[4] Williams to the Lord Admiral Buckingham, 27 July 1621—*Letters of Archbishop Williams with Documents Relating to Him* (ed. J. E. B. Mayor, 1866), p. 44.

[5] William Chesterman to Sir Edward Conway, 28 Aug. 1621—*S.P. Dom. Jas. I,* cxxii, 94.

best places in this church".[1] As for Laud, Abbot had given little indulgence to this man who was already anxious to exercise power within the Church.

As a result of the bishops' refusal to accept consecration at the hand of Abbot, the King referred the case to a Commission. Faced with this, Abbot took legal advice and engaged counsel. He had already shown some anxiety lest the peculiar verdict of the Coroner's inquest should not have been legally drawn up and had requested Lord Zouch to resummon the Coroner and jury to supply all defects.[2] Two days later his Counsel's advice had caused him to change his mind and he now considered that it would be less open to misrepresentation if the Coroner and jury were *not* recalled. He declared that, having a clear conscience and being anxious to do everything with decency, he did not wish to give his enemies any advantage.[3]

During this period of uncertainty Abbot spent more time in preaching than had hitherto been his custom; but this was perhaps unwise, for it was reported that he was "like to be in trouble" for it, "for a man in his case may not preach, say some civilians, before he has the King's pardon for his offence".[4] For a time he withdrew from affairs,[5] but after the middle of September he was frequently at Court where he was treated with marked kindliness. "My Lord of Canterbury", wrote an unknown correspondent to the Reverend Joseph Mead, "was on Tuesday at Court, kissed the King's hand, had private gracious words, held his place at Council; also went before his majesty to and from the chapel; dined there and departed cheerfully. So there is hope yet all will be well, though some seem to doubt."[6]

---

[1] *Cabala. Mysteries of State, in letters of the great Ministers of King James and King Charles* (1654), p. 56; cf. P. Heylyn, *Cyprianus Anglicus*, p. 88.

[2] Abbot to Lord Zouch, 5 Aug. 1621—*S.P. Dom. Jas. I*, cxxii, 61.

[3] Same to same, 7 Aug. 1621—*S.P. Dom. Jas. I*, cxxii, 63.

[4] *The Diary of Walter Yonge* (ed. G. Roberts, 1843), p. 43.

[5] Thomas Locke to Sir Dudley Carleton, 8 Sept. 1621—*S.P. Dom. Jas. I*, cxxii, 112.

[6] —— to the Revd Joseph Mead, 14 Sept. 1621—T. Birch, *Court and Times of James I* (1848), II, p. 274. Cf. also Thomas Locke to Carleton, 11 Sept. 1621 —*S.P. Dom. Jas. I*, cxxii, 117 ("The Archbishop of Canterbury has attended the King to the sermon, for the first time since the accident"); Same to same, 15 Sept. 1621—ibid., 129 ("The Archbishop of Canterbury has been again

The King's graciousness was a comfort to Abbot in his grief, for he felt keenly his position as "the talk of men".[1] Joseph Mead's correspondent had written that it was hoped "all will be well". A few days earlier the Earl of Leicester had told his son that the Earl of Pembroke and others at Court had said that "the Archbishop's business is like to go well" and he noted that the King and the Council continued to commit business to him.[2] On the other hand there were doubts, for the accident had "divided all great companies into *pro* and *con*, for or against the Archbishop's irregularity".[3] Ill fortune was prophesied for him.[4] and John Donne considered that he had little ground for any confidence.[5] Reports were circulated that he had been persuaded to resign his archbishopric and that he was to be granted a liberal pension. It was even rumoured that Lancelot Andrewes of Winchester was to succeed him and that Williams was to go to Winchester.[6] Later, talk went round that the King had withdrawn his graciousness and that when Abbot had sent to his Majesty to know whether he should attend him at Woodstock or elsewhere "it is said that he was prohibited to come to him anywhere, save at Whitehall".[7] Abbot's general unpopularity was no help to him in this crisis and his ill-wishers were ready enough to take advantage of his predicament and to put the worst construction upon it. Abbot himself saw his position as one which was "to the rejoicing of the Papist and insulting of the Puritan".[8] The Venetian Ambassador suggested that the Spanish party at Court did not neglect

with the King, and it is hoped all will now go well with him"); Same to same, 29 Sept. 1621—ibid., 152 ("The Archbishop of Canterbury is often at Court and well treated by the King").

[1] Abbot to Lord Zouch, 29 Aug. 1621—*S.P. Dom. Jas. I*, cxxii, 97.

[2] Robert, Earl of Leicester, to his son, Robert, Lord Viscount Lisle, 3 Sept. 1621—Arthur Collins, *Letters and Memorials of State in the Reigns of Queen Mary, Queen Elizabeth, James I, etc.* (1746), II, p. 353.

[3] T. Fuller, *Church History of Britain* (1655), Bk. x, sec. v, par. 14.

[4] Thomas Locke to Carleton, 8 Sept. 1621—*S.P. Dom. Jas. I*, cxxii, 112.

[5] John Donne to Sir Henry Goodyer, 30 Aug. 1621—E. W. Gosse, *Life and Letters of John Donne* (1899), II, p. 143.

[6] Revd Joseph Mead to Sir Martin Stuteville, 15 Sept. 1621—T. Birch, *Court and Times of James I* (1848), II, p. 275.

[7] Same to same, 22 Sept. 1621—op. cit., II, p. 276.

[8] Abbot to Lord Zouch, 29 Aug. 1621—*S.P. Dom. Jas. I*, cxxii, 97.

the opportunity which these events gave them to undermine the Archbishop.[1]

When the Commission was appointed in October it was found to consist of the Lord Keeper Williams (Bishop-elect of Lincoln), the Bishops of London, Winchester, and Rochester, the Bishops-elect of St David's and Exeter, Sir Henry Hobart (Chief Justice of the Common Pleas), Sir John Dodderidge (Judge of the King's Bench), Sir Henry Martin (Dean of Arches), and Dr Steward. In a letter to the Commission on 3 October the King outlined the facts of the accident and charged the Commission to "inform us concerning the nature of the case . . . and to certify us, what in your judgements the same may amount unto, either to an irregularity or otherwise, and lastly what means may be found to redress the same".[2] The situation was complicated by the fact that "the like had never happened in our Church nor in any other in the person of a Bishop and a Metropolitan, which made work for learned men to turn over their books".[3]

The Lord Keeper sent to Abbot a copy of the King's letter and informed him that the Commissioners were ready "to receive from your Grace (in writing) all the qualifying circumstances of the Fact (if any such there be) omitted in the Letter".[4] The Commission met at the College of Westminster on Saturday 13 October when three documents from the Archbishop were produced. The first was a copy of the Coroner's verdict, the second was a paper setting out circumstances of the accident which were not expressed in that verdict, and the third was a letter from Abbot himself requesting the Commission to "resolve what are the special Points of Law to be insisted upon", so that he might "with all convenient speed" cause his counsel to be ready to attend them. The Commissioners refused the request and the Lord Keeper wrote across the bottom of Abbot's letter: "To this letter we answered, that we had no warrant to hear Counsel; nor could we

[1] Venetian Ambassador to the Doge and Senate, 24 Sept. 1621—*S.P. Venetian*, xvii, no. 173.

[2] The King to the Commissioners, 3 Oct. 1621—*S.P. Dom. Jas. I,* cxxiii, 5; W. Cobbett, *Complete Collection of State Trials* (1809), II, pp. 1159 ff; *English Works of Sir Henry Spelman* (ed. E. Gibson, 1727), p. 121.

[3] J. Hacket, *Scrinia Reserata* (1693), p. 65.

[4] The Lord Keeper to Abbot, 5 Oct. 1621—W. Cobbett, op. cit.; *English Works of Sir Henry Spelman,* ibid.

in justice hear any, unless the Credit of the Church and the Honour of the King had their Counsel likewise on the other side."[1]

Rumour continued to spread. On the day the Commission met, Chamberlain told Carleton that he had heard that Andrewes of Winchester had refused the archbishopric and that the Archbishop of York was to have it, while London was to go to York and Williams to London. But Chamberlain wisely considered these to be "idle surmises", and he was encouraged in his scepticism by Abbot's own confidence in the issue, "not forebearing the Council Table, the Star Chamber, nor anything else he was wont to do".[2]

The Commission took its time in reaching a decision. On 27 October Chamberlain informed Carleton that the Commissioners were "very close in their proceedings" but that the Archbishop's fate lay in the King's hands alone.[3] On 10 November the members of the Commission delivered their opinion in a letter to the King. The report was not too unfavourable to the Archbishop. On the main question, whether he had incurred irregularity, the four lay members and the Bishop of Winchester (Andrewes) asserted that he had not, and the other five members said he had. In other words, the Commission was unable to give either a unanimous or a majority opinion on the main question. On the second question, whether Abbot's action might lead to scandal, Sir Henry Hobart, Dr Steward, and the Bishop of Winchester doubted whether it would, and the rest were of the opinion that "a Scandal may be taken by the Weak at home and the Malicious abroad", though most of them believed "there was no scandal given by the said Right Reverend Father". The most controversial question was the one concerning the procedure whereby the Archbishop should be reinstated. All the Commissioners agreed that it could be done only by the King, but some suggested that he should instruct four bishops to give formal absolution. Sir Henry Hobart, Dr Steward, and the Bishop of Winchester would have it done immediately by the

---

[1] Abbot to the Lord Keeper, 13 Oct. 1621—Lambeth Palace MSS., 943/77; *English Works of Sir Henry Spelman,* ibid.

[2] Chamberlain to Carleton, 13 Oct. 1621—McClure, II, p. 399.

[3] Chamberlain to Carleton, 27 Oct. 1621—*S.P. Dom. Jas. I,* cxxiii, 62.

King alone in the same Letters Patent which would contain his pardon, and others suggested that both courses should be followed. In the end it was left to the King to decide, although the opinion was expressed that "it is most fitting for the said Revd Father, both in regard to his Person and the Honour of the Church, to sue unto your most gracious Majesty for the said Dispensation . . . "[1]

It is worthy of some notice that on the first two questions Lancelot Andrewes, Bishop of Winchester, was out of step with the rest of his episcopal colleagues on the Commission, and this was commented upon at the time. Chamberlain told Carleton that it was said that Andrewes's advocacy—his "forceable reasons and arguments"—swayed the Commission to take a more lenient view than otherwise it might have done,[2] and Thomas Fuller wrote later that

> the Party, whom the Archbishop suspected his greatest Foe, proved his most firm and effectual Friend, even *Lancelot Andrewes Bishop of Winchester*: For when several Bishops inveighed against the irregularity of the Archbishop, laying as much (if not more) guilt, on the act, than it would bear, He mildly checked them: *Brethren* (said he) *be not too busy to condemn any for Uncanonicals according to the strictness thereof, lest we render ourselves in the same condition. Besides we all know*, Canones, qui dicunt lapsos post actam poenitentiam ad clericatum non esse restituendos, de rigore loquuntur disciplinae, non injiciunt desperationem indulgentiae.[3]

The surprise which these comments reveal is understandable, for Andrewes had no cause to champion Abbot on personal grounds, and in outlook, theology, and churchmanship they had nothing in common. He cannot have been satisfied with an archiepiscopal way of life which led to homicide in the hunting field. It would appear almost certain that his leniency was due, as Heylyn later suggested, to certain consequences which he feared would follow if Abbot was deprived. Chief among

---

[1] J. Hacket, *Scrinia Reserata* (1693), pp. 67 ff; *The English Works of Sir Henry Spelman*, ibid.

[2] Chamberlain to Carleton, 10 Nov. 1621—McClure, II, p. 406.

[3] T. Fuller, *Church History of Britain* (1655), Bk. x. sec. v, par. 16.

these was the possibility that Williams would succeed him, and Andrewes was unlikely to regard Williams as other than an unsatisfactory and dangerous head of the Church.[1]

On Sunday 11 November Williams's consecration took place "with great festivity" in Westminster Abbey. The ceremony was performed by the Bishops of London, Worcester, Ely, Oxford, and Llandaff, acting under a commission from Abbot "who has not yet meddled in such things".[2] The next day the King expressed to Abbot his displeasure that three other bishops (Salisbury, St David's, and Exeter) had not been consecrated at the same time, "the Parliament being so near at hand".[3] In a letter of explanation to the King, Abbot said that it had not been possible to consecrate all the bishops on the same day because he had not known until the previous Wednesday that Williams had decided to be consecrated on the Sunday. By that time it was found to be too late to have the necessary documents prepared for the other three bishops. One of the main reasons for this was that the new Bishop of Exeter had not yet received the certificate of his election. Abbot concluded by assuring the King that he had given order for the other consecrations to be held on the next Sunday, and that in all this there had been "no default in me, to whom it was indifferent whether this consecration had been on Sunday last or were to be on Sunday next".[4] On 18 November the three bishops were consecrated in the chapel of London House by the Bishops of London, Worcester, Ely, Oxford, Llandaff, and Chichester under a commission from the Archbishop.

In accordance with the advice of the Commission which had reported on his irregularity, Abbot applied to the King for his dispensation and James directed a fresh Commission to the Bishops of Lincoln, London, Winchester, Norwich, Lichfield and Coventry, and Bath and Wells, to "dispense with any irregularity".[5] The Commission met on 22 November and granted dispensation, so that the Archbishop was fully restored to the exercise of his functions, and the King "by his Broad-Seal absolved

---

[1] Peter Heylyn, *Cyprianus Anglicus* (1668), p. 88.

[2] Locke to Carleton, 16 Nov. 1621—*S.P. Dom. Jas. I,* cxxiii, 107.

[3] Locke to Carleton, 17 Nov. 1621—*S.P. Dom. Jas. I,* cxxiii, 110.

[4] Abbot to the King, 13 Nov. 1621—*For escue Papers* (ed. S. R. Gardiner, 1871), p. 164.

[5] *S.P. Dom. Jas. I,* cxxiii, 118.

WILLIAM LAUD
From a portrait in the National Portrait Gallery

GEORGE ABBOT
From a portrait in the Gorhambury Collection

the Archbishop from all Irregularity, Scandal, or Infamation, pronouncing him to be capable to use all Metropolitical Authority, as if that sinistrous Contingency in spilling blood had never been done".[1]

Thus the affair ended, but its effect upon Abbot and his reputation remained. It brought him increased obloquy from his enemies, and if he received graciousness from the King in contrast to the black looks he had suffered during the last *cause célèbre* in which he was involved, it did not compensate for the great scar which the tragedy left in his heart. For the remainder of his life he observed a monthly fast on the day on which the event occurred. "The Keeper's *death* was the Archbishop's *mortification*."[2]

NOTE

John Hacket described the case of Abbot's homicide as one "which made work for learned men to turn over their books".[3] Even the Sorbonne was invited to express its opinion and three times its professors discussed the question and condemned the Archbishop.[4] At home Sir Henry Saville, an old acquaintance of Abbot's and a contemporary of his at Oxford, called on Sir Edward Coke and put to him the question, "*Whether may a Bishop hunt in a Park by the Laws of the Realm?*" Coke's reply was that "*he may hunt by the Laws of the Realm by this very token, That there is an old Law . . . that a Bishop, when dying, is to leave his pack of Dogs . . . to the King's free use and disposal.*"[5]

The most extended arguments on the case are contained in two documents written during October 1621. The first of these was entitled, "A Short Apology for Archbishop Abbot, touching the death of Peter Hawkins. By an Unknown hand".[6] The writer made the theological point that the homicide was not a human accident but an act of divine providence, which no man can absolutely prevent: and no calling—not even that of the priest— "is free from that which God will have accomplished". He quoted

[1] John Hacket, *Scrinia Reserata* (1692), p. 68.
[2] T. Fuller, *Church History of Britain* (1655), Bk. x, sec. v, par. 17.
[3] Op. cit., p. 65.   [4] J. Hacket, ibid.
[5] T. Fuller, *Church History of Britain* (1655), Bk. x, sec. v, par. 15; W. Cobbett, *Complete Collection of State Trials* (1809), II, p. 1164.
[6] Printed in *The English Works of Sir Henry Spelman* (ed. E. Gibson, 1727), pp. 105 ff.

Old Testament examples of priests who shed blood and continued their priestly functions. He then turned to the legal aspects of Abbot's case. The Law, he said, excuses a man from irregularity in such accidental killings provided that the occupation he is engaged in when the accident occurs is not in itself unlawful, and provided also that due care is taken that no hurt shall befall. Abbot was engaged in no unlawful pursuit, for there is no law against hunting; like the rest of the party, he took due care— "never man being more solicitous thereof, than he evermore was".

But Abbot was a clergyman, and it had been asserted that hunting, while lawful in itself, was forbidden to clergymen. The authority quoted for this opinion was the canon *De Clerico Venatore,* but the Apologist argued that the canon does not apply either in this particular case nor to any case in England. He gave six reasons why it did not apply in this particular case, two of the most relevant being that the canon forbids hunting *cum canibus aut Accipitribus,* whereas neither were used at Bramshill, and that it forbids hunting *Voluptatis causa,* whereas Abbot was hunting for his health's sake and the canon contains no prohibition of hunting for such a purpose. More fundamentally, the canon (the Apologist argued) had no legal force in England anyhow, for since the Reformation no canon which is contrary to the laws of the realm or the King's prerogative can be legally enforced. The canon in question was contrary to both. It was contrary to the *Charta de Foresta,* which granted archbishops and bishops liberty to hunt, and to an Act of Richard II's reign, which permitted certain clergy to keep hunting-dogs. Moreover, hunting by bishops in their parks had continued to this day without scruple or question, and the Apologist cited examples. The conclusion was clear: "That howsoever the canon may touch Bishops and Clergymen beyond the Seas, it meddleth not with the Bishops of England. . . . So that it doth . . . arise that there is no danger of Irregularity in the Lord Archbishop's case, either towards himself or other men."

On 8 October this Apology was sent to Sir Henry Spelman, the eminent lawyer and historian, who returned an Answer[1] to

[1] "An Answer to the Foregoing Apology", by Sir Henry Spelman. Printed in *The English Works of Sir Henry Spelman* (ed. E. Gibson, 1727), pp. 110 ff.

it on 19 October. This document is strained in its argument and harsh in its severity. The Apologist's array of Old Testament examples of priests shedding blood was countered by the true observation that the New Testament has superseded the Old. In the New Testament Jesus had told Peter to put up his sword, and on this precedent the law of the Church was that clergymen were forbidden to shed blood. Spelman then cited five examples of truly accidental homicide by clergymen, such as the case of the priest who, having tolled a bell which fell and killed a boy, was allowed to continue his functions. But in all the cases cited there was no *intention* to kill. In Abbot's case, however, although there was no intention to hurt a man, the whole purpose of the hunt was to kill a beast, and that was "killing". The homicide was thus not truly accidental. Moreover, Spelman continued, it was not true to say that Abbot took due care, for he was a very bad shot with the cross-bow and ought, therefore, never to have handled one.

With regard to the Apologist's objections against the applicability of the canon, *De Clerico Venatore,* Spelman asserted that if the Apologist had continued his quotation it would have been clear that it covered "all instruments used in Hunting" and not only hunting *cum canibus aut Accipitribus.* It was also nonsense to maintain that hunting could be of use for health. "What *Action* or *Recreation* belonging to health is there, in letting off a Cross-bow; wherein neither Head, Hand, nor Foot, no, not the nimblest member of the Body (the Eye) stirreth all that while?" Again, the canon *does* possess legal force in England for it is *not* contrary to Statute Law nor to the royal prerogative. The examples cited by the Apologist—said Spelman—were misconceived. The canon does not contradict the *Charta de Foresta,* for the latter does not say that bishops shall hunt. Here Spelman became very casuistical. The *Charta,* he said, spoke of permitting bishops "to take a deer". He maintained that this phrase meant that they might do it "by the hands of their officers and servants". As for the Statute of Richard II's reign, that was couched in the negative rather than the positive. Finally, although the bishops had parks those were not granted them to hunt in, for they cannot use the parks otherwise than the laws and canons of the Church permit. Thus the legal argument made it clear that Abbot, in killing a keeper, was irregular.

It is not known why the Apology and its answer were drawn up, but it may be that they were intended for the use of the Commission. They serve as illustrations of the lines of argument adopted by the protagonists in this strange and unprecedented case.

8

"In Exitu Israel"

Fall into the hands of God, not into the hands of Spain.

From ALFRED, LORD TENNYSON, The Revenge

ALTHOUGH THE homicide and its consequences were heart-rending to Abbot himself, they were but a summer interlude in far more momentous affairs of State, which were to lead to the crisis of the reign of James I. Parliament had been adjourned in June, and a few days before the Commission granted Abbot his dispensation it reassembled. Most of the interest and tension of the session centred on the uneasy relation between the King and the Commons, for by Christmas the gulf between the two was wider than ever. Abbot sat in the calmer atmosphere of the House of Lords, where business was free from the critical issues which occupied the Commons. He was present at every sitting of the House and served on innumerable Committees, including one dealing with the vexed question of Monopolies.[1] Shortly before Parliament adjourned for the Christmas recess the Commons drew up a protestation declaring their privileges, which so angered the King that, rather than endure such "insolence", he dissolved Parliament.

Early in the new year (1622) Abbot took part in the examination of the notorious Marco Antonio de Dominis, Archbishop of Spalato, after his re-conversion to Rome. He had had dealings with de Dominis ever since the latter had fled to this country in 1616 after he had asserted in a book that successive Popes had added new and unwarrantable articles to the creed. As early as December 1615 Abbot had told Sir Dudley Carleton that de Dominis must not "expect great entertainment in England", but at the same time he offered him "a private life in a university"

---

[1] *Journals of the House of Lords,* II.

and £100 a year.[1] Over a year later he had not arrived and Abbot sent word through Carleton that if de Dominis was still resolved to come "his portion will suffice him to live at one of the universities, without state, . . . and sometimes attending the King in London".[2] Eventually he came and received an enthusiastic welcome. Benefices were granted to him and court was paid to him by the highest in the land. He visited Oxford and Cambridge, and in August 1617 Abbot was writing to Sir Thomas Lake on his behalf to seek an interview for him with the King.[3] King James gladly received him and presented him to the Deanery of Windsor and the Mastership of the Savoy. In October Abbot took him to Eton College, where Sir Henry and Lady Saville "loaded him with caresses". Nevertheless he was not a free agent and was required to remain in London, where, however, he was well treated.[4]

"De Dominis, however, was vain, ignorant of the world, quarrelsome, and avaricious. He looked in vain for the English Church to seek his guidance and leadership. Moreover, he was disappointed and dissatisfied with the Church of England itself, and once more he turned his eyes to Rome. In January 1622 he announced his intention to return."[5] James I was much angered by this *volte-face* and ordered Abbot and certain other bishops to speak and dispute with Spalato and to inquire into the motive of his conduct.[6] In March Abbot was a member of the formal Commission which examined de Dominis. At the King's command he delivered a long Latin speech in which he deplored de Dominis's inconsistency in coming to England as a convert from Rome and now desiring to return, having for that purpose held correspondence with the Pope without the King's knowledge. After de Dominis had made answer—"rather a shuffling excuse than a just defence"[7]—the Archbishop ordered him, in the King's

---

[1] Abbot to Carleton, 15 Dec. 1614—*S.P. Dom. Jas. I*, lxxviii, 72.

[2] Same to same, 16 Feb. 1615—ibid., lxxx, 29.

[3] Abbot to Sir Thomas Lake, 4 Aug. 1617—ibid., xciii, 2.

[4] Archbishop of Spalato to Sir Dudley Carleton, 16 Oct. 1617—ibid., xciii, 128.

[5] Paul A. Welsby, *Lancelot Andrewes*, p. 159.

[6] *S.P. Venetian*, xvii, no. 232—11 Feb. 1622.

[7] Fuller, op. cit., Bk. x, sec. vi, par. 11.

name, to depart the realm within twenty days.[1] After his departure
de Dominis attacked Abbot severely, and a year later John
Chamberlain had heard that he still "railed continually on my
Lord of Canterbury and at every word calls him *homicida*".[2]

Abbot and the King were both becoming concerned with the
unsettled state of the Church. Every day they heard of "defec-
tions from our Religion, both to Popery and Anabaptism, or
other points of Separatism".[3] They laid much of the blame for
this at the door of the "lightness, affectedness and unprofitable-
ness of that kind of preaching, which hath been of late years too
much taken up in Court, University, City, and County".[4] As an
attempt to remedy the situation the King issued a series of
"Directions concerning Preachers", which he ordered the Archbishop to enforce and to command all bishops to send to their
clergy.[5] Abbot obeyed these instructions and in a letter to the
Bishop of Lincoln commended them as indicating the King's
"princely care for the orderly preaching of Christ crucified, of
obedience to the higher powers, and of a Christian life, and not
that every young man should take exorbitant liberty to teach
what he listeth, to the disquiet of the King, Church and Commonwealth".[6]

James's grotesque infatuation for the Spanish Match was
rapidly assuming pathological proportions. All through 1622 he
pushed hard at the marriage but found the going exceedingly
heavy because the Pope was reluctant to grant the necessary
dispensation that was required to enable a Roman Catholic to
marry a Protestant. The reason for His Holiness's hesitation was
his advisers' insistence that further concessions, including the
repeal of the penal laws, should be extracted from England.
A climax was reached when Prince Charles took a personal hand

[1] Peter Heylyn, *Cyprianus Anglicus* (1719 ed.), p. 103.
[2] Chamberlain to Carleton, 4 Jan. 1623—McClure, II, p. 470.
[3] Abbot to (?)Sir Walter Boswell, 4 Sept. 1622—Add. MSS. (British
Museum), 6394, ff. 29-30.
[4] Ibid.
[5] The King to the Archbishop of Canterbury, 4 Aug. 1622—*S.P. Dom.
Jas. I,* cxxxii, 85.
[6] Archbishop of Canterbury to Bishop of Lincoln, 12 Aug. 1622—*S.P.
Dom. Jas. I,* cxxxii, 93.

in the negotiations and, accompanied by Buckingham, set forth in February 1623 on his expedition to Spain to woo his future bride. The reaction of Court and people to this foolhardy action was one of anger and consternation. Abbot, together with the other anti-Spanish councillors, was convinced of the evi¹; which would follow. In March he was ill with gout and was unable to preach at the funeral of the Earl of Exeter,[1] but had recovered in time to preach before the King on Palm Sunday.[2] He was present at the meeting of the Council held in July to give consent to the Spanish Marriage treaty. Such was James's obsession with the alliance that he was prepared to accept terms which were humiliating both to the nation and to his own sovereignty. They included the granting of freedom of worship to Papists and a promise never to reimpose the penal laws. He laid the treaty before the Council and insisted, with tears, that it be approved lest the Prince in Spain should be made a prisoner. Abbot boldly led the way in asking inconvenient questions, and (according to Joseph Mead) avowed that he would lose his life rather than ever give consent to it.[3] This opposition from Abbot angered the King, who ordered him to sign. In the end he complied with the royal demand, although (according to Hacket) he publicly declared in a sermon at Whitehall his personal distrust of the treaty.[4]

A few days afterwards there began to circulate in London a pamphlet in the form of a letter from Archbishop Abbot to King James. This document condemned in vigorous and outspoken terms the King's toleration of Popery, the Prince's journey to Spain, and the King's indifference to Parliament. "By your act [i.e. in signing the treaty]", the letter declared, "you labour to set up that most damnable and heretical doctrine of the Church of Rome, the whore of Babylon." On the Prince's journey, the letter warned "the drawers of him into that action so dangerous to himself, so desperate to the kingdom", that they would not be permitted to "pass away unquestioned and unpunished". Finally, the toleration proposed "cannot be done without Parlia-

[1] Chamberlain to Carleton, 8 March 1623—McClure, II, p. 483.
[2] Same to same, 19 April 1623—S.P. Dom. Jas. I, cxliii, 22.
[3] The Revd Joseph Mead to Sir Martin Stuteville, 29 July 1623—T. Birch, Court and Times of James I (1848), II, p. 416.
[4] J. Hacket, Scrinia Reserata, p. 143.

ment, unless your Majesty will let your subjects see that you now take unto yourself a liberty to throw down the laws of the land at your pleasure". The letter concluded: "Thus in discharge of my duty towards God, to your Majesty, and the place of my calling, I have taken humble leave to deliver my conscience. Now, Sir, do what you please with me."[1]

The appearance of the letter created a furore. Abbot at once denied all knowledge of it and begged the King to punish the author,[2] but although search was made the author was never discovered. There can be little doubt that Abbot's denial was sincere, for there are good reasons against his authorship of the document. In the first place its tone was far too vehement and threatening for Abbot. Secondly, having signed the treaty it is unlikely that he would expose himself to disfavour by such a tactless and public demonstration. Moreover, there is a wide variety of texts, and in two contemporary copies[3] the document is described as a "speech", which lends additional weight to the belief that it was a forgery. The author may have been an enemy of Abbot who hoped to disgrace the Archbishop, or he may have been a supporter who was over-enthusiastic.

The letter placed Abbot in a difficult position. Apparently he earned the disapproval of the Court by his hesitation in making his denial public. This reluctance is perhaps understandable, for the sentiments contained in the letter coincided with Abbot's own convictions, and it was difficult to disown the letter without giving the impression that he was also renouncing the opinions expressed in it. The letter circulated so widely and did so much harm that it was suggested that Abbot should direct "the preachers about London and the Bishops in their several dioceses to publish His Grace's detestation of the paper and its author".[4] The following day Secretary Conway reported that further circulation of the letter had been forbidden,[5] but as late as

---

[1] 8 Aug. 1623—*S.P. Dom. Jas. I*, cl, 55–7; Add. MSS. (British Museum), 4108; T. Fuller, op. cit., Bk. v, pp. 545–9.

[2] Venetian Ambassador to the Doge and Senate, 11 Aug. 1623—*S.P. Venetian*, xviii, no. 107.   [3] Tanner MSS., lxxiii, 24.

[4] Secretary Calvert to Secretary Conway, 8 Aug. 1623—*S.P. Dom. Jas. I*, cl, 54.

[5] Secretary Conway to Secretary Calvert, 9 Aug. 1623—*S.P. Dom. Jas. I*, cl, 64.

4 September he was inquiring why the forgery had not been publicly disavowed.[1]

Abbot was far nearer to seeing the accomplishment of his wishes about the Spanish marriage than he could have ever foreseen, for, although nothing now appeared to stand in the way of the marriage, it never took place. Prince Charles had begun to awake from his dream, to resent the treatment he was receiving in Spain, and to perceive the emptiness of Spanish promises. In September he threatened to leave. The Spaniards took him at his word and expedited his departure. Leaving behind a proxy for his marriage he landed in England on 5 October amid scenes of heartfelt rejoicing. Abbot was triumphant. He met the Prince on his arrival in London at Lambeth stairs and had him conveyed in his own barge to York House.[2] England went mad with joy; at a solemn service in St Paul's Cathedral the psalm *In exitu Israel*[3] was sung as an anthem of thanksgiving.

Buckingham, resentful at his treatment in Spain, was now completely opposed to the Spanish marriage. After some initial hesitation, Prince Charles supported him, and faced with their united front James capitulated. He was pressed to demand from Spain an understanding regarding the restitution of the Palatinate, and this resulted in the ending in Spain of all preparations for the marriage by proxy. The Prince and Buckingham next urged a meeting of Parliament; opposition to the proposal was overcome, and the Houses met in February 1624. Abbot attended regularly and played a more prominent and important part in its business than in any other session of any other Parliament, largely because its most important work was concerned with breaking off relations with Spain—and the Archbishop could be relied upon to devote his time and his abilities to forward a task so congenial to his personal convictions.

Lords and Commons at once turned their attention to the Spanish treaties. Buckingham, with certain reservations, recited the whole history of the marriage negotiations. A motion in Buckingham's favour was carried in the Lords on 27 February,[4]

---

[1] Same to same, 4 Sept. 1623—ibid., clii, 6.

[2] Francis Ryves to Dr Usher, 8 Oct. 1623—J. Nichols, *Progresses*, IV, p. 927. [3] Ps. 114.

[4] *Journals of the House of Lords*, II—27 Feb. 1624.

when Abbot in a speech thanked God "for clearing of these mists".[1] In the afternoon the Lords debated the treaties themselves and Abbot spoke again. He advised his hearers to take care to speak nothing which might be dishonourable to the King of Spain personally, but to confine their criticism to the King's officers. He maintained that this country had been deceived by Spain many times and, as they must "judge of things to come by that which is passed", it would be expedient for the treaties to be condemned on the ground that it would be impossible to repose further confidence in Spain.[2] In the meantime the Spanish Ambassador had complained against the terms Buckingham had used in speaking of the King of Spain. Abbot was appointed by the Lords to open business on their behalf at a conference of a committee of both Houses to investigate these charges against Buckingham, and he later reported to the House that it was agreed that the charges were unjustified.[3] On 2 March he was a member of another committee of the Lords appointed to attend the King with a petition from both Houses recommending that the negotiations with Spain should be broken off. He later informed that House that the petition had been delivered and that the King had "returned a grave, gracious, and wise answer".[4]

One of the points which the King made in his reply was that, although he would not own "one furrow of land in England, Scotland, or Ireland without restitution of the Palatinate", he could not declare war until he knew that he had the financial backing to support it. Consequently on 11 March Abbot was nominated to a committee to confer with the Commons "about the state of the King's affairs", and the following day he reported that the conference had unanimously agreed to assist the King, "whensoever His Majesty shall be pleased to declare himself touching the breaking of the two treaties with Spain". On the thirteenth it was agreed that the Archbishop in the name of both Houses should present an address to the King embodying the ideas expressed in debate. Abbot showed a certain anxiety to obtain the House's approval of a speech he proposed to make to

[1] *Notes on Debates in the House of Lords, 1624 and 1626* (ed. S. R. Gardiner, 1879), p. 3.

[2] Ibid., pp. 5 f.   [3] Ibid., p. 16.

[4] *Journals of the House of Lords*, II, 2 and 8 March.

the King before reading the address—"a little preface of ceremony and duty first to his Majesty".[1] He suggested that he should say: "We are come again the second time from his faithful subjects the Lords and Commons." He would add that "we acknowledge ourselves bound to God for such a King over us that will hear us speak in matters of moment", and he proposed to conclude by alluding to the indignities being suffered by Princess Elizabeth in the Palatinate, "in consideration whereof we humbly present a speech in writing . . . and desire to read the same". The Lords agreed that a preamble on those lines would be appropriate.[2]

The following day the Archbishop waited on the King at Whitehall, made his speech, and read the address from Parliament. In his reply the King expressed offence at the condemnation of the Spaniards' insincerity contained in the address, of which he was not yet convinced. Furthermore, he pressed for more definite information about the amount of money Parliament was prepared to vote.[3] This carping utterance was understood by many to imply that there would be no war after all. Abbot was absent from the House on the following day,[4] and it was said that he had been so discouraged by the King's reply that he was ill.[5] On 22 March he was on the Lords' committee to confer with the Commons about the financial problem, and when he returned to the House he reported that the Commons had voted three subsidies and three fifteenths, but had accompanied the resolution with an address declaring explicitly that the money was for "the support of the war which is likely to ensue". The Lords associated themselves with the address and appointed Abbot to deliver it to the King.[6] To this address the King replied by declaring that the Spanish treaties were dissolved. This was the signal for another outburst of public rejoicing after the anxiety of years.

The Spanish treaties had done much to exacerbate anti-Papist feeling in England, and immediately they had been dissolved Parliament turned to the question of the enforcement of the

---

[1] *Notes on Debates, 1624 and 1626* (ed. S. R. Gardiner), p. 31.

[2] Ibid., p. 32.   [3] *S.P. Dom. Jas. I,* clx, 77.

[4] *Journals of the House of Lords,* II, 15 March 1624.

[5] Edward Nicholas to John Nicholas, March 1624—*S.P. Dom. Jas. I,* clx, 81.

[6] *Journal of the House of Lords,* II, 22 March 1614.

penal laws against the recusants. Abbot was a leading member of the Lords' committee which conferred with the Commons on several occasions about the matter, and on 5 April when the Lords considered a petition which the Commons had drawn up requesting the King to enforce the existing penal laws, Abbot spoke strongly in its favour. He regarded it as "the motion of the Spirit of God to [have] put this into the minds of the Commons. . . . If Religion be neglected, no blessing [is] to be expected." He gave three reasons why the proposed action against the recusants was a wise one. First, because of "the insolency of the adverse parties"—and he cited the case of the Bishop of Chalcedon who had openly told of his public activities in London and Staffordshire, which had included a number of confirmations, "contrary to the jurisdiction of the Crown"; secondly, because of the great influx of Papists from the Continent; and thirdly, because the Papists are going "by thousands to mass, and to the great offence of the people".[1]

Abbot was involved in the impeachment of the Earl of Middlesex, the Lord Treasurer, who had been accused of corruption. He was on the committee which drew up the heads of the charges against the accused,[2] and on 12 May he made a speech in the Lords in the course of which he asserted that the Lord Treasurer was "in no way to be excused", for he had committed the crime of neglecting that which belonged to the King.[3] Later in the discussion Abbot said that Middlesex, finding that men needed his help and favour, had "palliated a bribe with a bargain". His was a "foul crime", deserving a heavy censure.[4] The next day the Lords debated what would be a fitting punishment for such a crime and Abbot suggested that a fine of £50,000 would be appropriate for "an Earl of high honour and rich" who had stooped to such corruption.[5] This was the amount of the fine which was actually imposed, in addition to deprivation of office, imprisonment, and prohibition against sitting in Parliament. On 15 May Abbot was among those who waited upon the King to acquaint him with the judgement.[6]

---

[1] *Notes on Debates* (ed. S. R. Gardiner), p. 53.
[2] *Journals of the House of Lords,* II.
[3] *Notes on Debates* (ed. S. R. Gardiner), p. 75.
[4] Ibid., p. 79.　　[5] Ibid., p. 90.　　[6] *Journals of the House of Lords,* II.

No sooner had the Earl of Middlesex been disposed of than Abbot was faced with a problem of some difficulty. Richard Montague, Rector of Stamford Rivers in Essex, published a controversial book with the engaging title of *A New Gag for an Old Goose*,[1] in which he refused to condemn certain Romish practices and in which he reduced to a minimum the differences between the doctrines of Rome and England. He refused to accept the Calvinist doctrine of predestination or to regard the Church of Rome as Antichrist. Two clergymen complained to a committee of the Commons about the publication of such opinions and the Commons referred the objections to the Archbishop of Canterbury. Now the theological views expressed by Montague were anathema to Abbot, whose sympathies were wholly with the objectors; but he had to tread warily for it appeared possible that the King might have his own ideas on the subject of the controversy. Abbot therefore asked the King what course he had better follow and James suggested that the Archbishop should examine Montague. When the latter appeared before him, Abbot addressed to him the following admonition.

Mr Montague, you profess you hate Popery, and no way incline to Arminianism. You see what disturbance is grown in the Church and the Parliament House by the book by you lately put forth. Be of no occasion of scandal or offence; and therefore this is my advice unto you. Go home, review over your book. It may be divers things have slipped you, which, upon better advice, you will reform. If anything be said too much, take it away; if anything be too little, add unto it; if anything be obscure, explain it; but do not wed yourself to your own opinion, and remember we must give account of our ministry unto Christ.[2]

Montague ignored this advice. Instead he sought an audience of the King, who displayed complete sympathy with him and granted him permission to publish a second work, which was entitled *Appello Caesarem*.[3] This was partly a reiteration of the position set forth in the work for which he had just been admon-

[1] Written as a reply to *The Gag for the New Gospel*, by a Papist who identified the teaching of the Church of England with Calvinism.

[2] Quoted S. R. Gardiner, *History of England, 1603–42* (1883–4), V, p. 354.

[3] 1625.

ished. He attacked the Calvinists and the English Puritans and he vindicated his own claim to be the exponent of the true doctrine of the Church of England. Although the work was furiously attacked, it was in fact a vindication of his teaching from any Roman tendencies. Once again Parliament was aroused and the Commons sent a deputation to Abbot to discover what steps he had taken to deal with Montague. "The deputation found him much vexed. After telling them all that had happened, he complained that he had not even been informed of the intended publication of the second book till it was actually in the press. As, however, he had no legal jurisdiction over Montague on the mere complaint of the House of Commons, all that he could say was that he would gladly give his judgement upon the *Appello Caesarem* whenever he should be 'orderly directed to it'."[1]

Having failed to elicit Abbot's unofficial support, the Commons referred the matter to a Parliamentary committee, which reported unfavourably on 7 July and accused Montague of dishonouring the King, of displaying contempt for Parliament, and of sowing dissension in Church and State. King Charles, who had now succeeded his father, found Montague's theology wholly acceptable and, as a gesture against the Commons, made him a royal chaplain. It is very significant that Abbot now dropped out of the affair and he was not numbered among those bishops who discussed the case further in January 1626.[2] The "Montague affair" petered out and two years later he was appointed Bishop of Chichester.

The fact that Abbot's connection with Montague's case came to an abrupt end is some indication that the men who counted in the early years of the new reign were Buckingham and Laud. Even before King James died the influence of these two figures was greatly increasing. In old age James lost all control over his son and his favourite, and Buckingham's chaplain, Laud, shared in the fortunes of his patron. Abbot began to feel the effects of the power of these two men. The growing pride of Buckingham so "dismayed" him that he fell sick and was obliged to absent himself from Court. In a letter to Sir Dudley Carleton in August 1624 he expressed his regret at the "rubs" which all suffer alike

[1] S. R. Gardiner, op. cit., V, pp. 354 f.
[2] Harleian MSS. (British Museum), 700, f. 193.

who do "not stoop sail to that castle", and he added that success could not always be guaranteed by subservience. "At the moment", he concluded, "he stands higher than ever, and I cannot tell what presages."[1]

The Duke's chaplain was Abbot's old antagonist. In 1624 there occurred an incident which served only to deepen their mutual hostility. Laud suggested to Buckingham that the subsidies granted to the Crown by the clergy in Convocation, which were a heavy burden on the poorer benefices, should be paid by instalments. Buckingham approved of the proposal and promised to use his good offices to prepare the King and the Prince for the passing of it. Laud next placed his scheme before Bishop Neile of Durham and Bishop Williams of Lincoln. The latter regarded it as "the best office that was done for the Church this seven years", and they both persuaded him to approach the Archbishop. When he did so and had outlined his scheme Abbot was extremely angry and asked "what I had to do to make any suit for the Church. Told me, never any Bishop attempted the like any time, nor would any but myself have done it. That I had given the Church such a wound, in speaking to any Lord of the Laity about it, as I could never make whole again." Laud defended himself and declared that he considered that he had done a good office for the Church and that his betters thought so too. If the Archbishop thought otherwise, he was sorry to have offended him. What he had done, he concluded, was out of consideration of the "many poor vicars abroad in the country, who must sink under their subsidies in a year". That being his intention, he hoped that his "error (if it were one) was pardonable". So they parted.[2]

Use has been made of this incident to suggest that Abbot cared little about the plight of the poorer parochial clergy. The indifference of Abbot, who had had no experience of parochial life, has been contrasted unfavourably with the concern of Laud. It would be nearer the truth to see in the incident a manifestation of such intense antipathy on the part of Abbot towards Laud and Laud's theological position that the merits of Laud's case were lost sight of in his dislike of its author. The vehemence of

[1] Abbot to Carleton, 18 Aug. 1624—S.P. Dom. Jas. I, clxxi, 59.

[2] W. Laud, Works (ed. W. Scott and J. Bliss, 1847–60), III, p. 151; P. Heylyn, Cyprianus Anglicus, p. 119.

Abbot's language was a measure of his hypersensitivity at Laud's growing influence at Court and at his efforts to attain influence in ecclesiastical affairs as well. When faced with Laud's scheme, Abbot was not prepared to give it consideration—not because he was indifferent to the troubles of the poorer clergy, but because he objected violently to the author of it on personal grounds and because to have acceded to the plan would inevitably have brought Laud a popularity and importance which were the last things which Abbot was prepared to allow him. It needs also to be remembered, when considering this interview, that Laud possessed neither tact nor a soft tongue.

Such was Abbot's dislike of Laud that he attempted to exclude him from the High Commission, although every other bishop living in or near London and a number who lived farther afield were put in. Laud, however, appealed to Buckingham, who was able to secure his inclusion.[1]

Archbishop Abbot was instrumental in the founding of Pembroke College, Oxford, in 1624. Thomas Tisdale, a grazier and a native of Abingdon, had died in 1610 and had left the sum of £5,000 to Abbot, Sir John Bennet, his own nephew, and Dr Airy, Provost of Queen's, to "maintain thirteen scholars in Balliol College in the University of Oxford, if they may be conveniently placed and entertained", and if not, then in University College, or, failing that, in some other college.[2] The choice of colleges clearly shows Abbot's influence, for he had been Master of University College and he had also preserved a strong affection for his own college, Balliol. In 1616 he had given the sum of £100 to the Master and Fellows of Balliol, and three years later he had spent money upon repairing old books in the college library and purchasing new ones.[3] Now in 1624 the Master and Fellows of Balliol entered into negotiations with the Corporation of Abingdon, for Tisdale's scheme was closely connected with Abingdon School. The sum of £300 changed hands, but Balliol rashly spent the money before the negotiations were completed. Caesar's Buildings were erected to provide accommodation for the

---

[1] W. Laud, *Works*, VI, p. 243; P. Heylyn, *Cyprianus Anglicus*, p. 117.

[2] *Balliofergus, or a Commentary upon the Foundation, Founders and Affairs of Balliol College* (1668), pp. 86 f.

[3] H. W. C. Davis, *Balliol College* (1899), p. 117.

scholars and six of the scholars themselves were installed. In 1623, however, Richard Wightwick had augmented the Tisdale foundation so liberally that it was now felt that the total endowment justified the foundation of a separate college. The result was the foundation of Pembroke College and Abbot appears to have been quite willing to acquiesce in the transaction. Later, the Fellows of Pembroke sued Balliol for the repayment of the £300 which it had received. "The treasury was quite empty, and the demand would have brought them to bankruptcy if Abbot had not paid the whole sum out of his own pocket."[1]

[1] H. W. C. Davis, op. cit., p. 127; see C. E. Mallet, *A History of the University of Oxford* (1924), II, pp. 272, 277.

9

"Dr Sibthorpe's contemptible Treatise"

The virtue of Prosperity is temperance, the virtue of Adversity is fortitude: which in morals is the more heroical virtue. . . . Prosperity is not without many fears and distastes; and Adversity is not without comforts and hopes. . . . Certainly virtue is like precious odours, most fragrant when they are increased or crushed: for Prosperity doth best discover vice, but Adversity doth best discover virtue.

FRANCIS BACON, *Essay: Of Adversity*

" O N THE morning of Sunday 27 March a little before noon, 'his lords and servants kneeling on one side, his archbishops, bishops and others of his chaplains on the other side of his bed, without pangs or convulsions at all, Solomon slept'."[1] Allowance must be made for the aura of piety which surrounds the death-beds of monarchs, for in actual fact the death of King James was horrible. There is, however, no doubt that he made a godly end, and as the time for his departing drew near he called for Bishop Lancelot Andrewes. The latter was confined to his own house by illness and his place was taken by Abbot and Williams.

The death of James I was also the death-knell of Abbot's influence in Church and State. His fortunes had been declining since the homicide in 1621, but the conversion of the Government to an anti-Spanish policy had brought him a brief moment of triumph. By the irony of fortune, however, the adoption of that policy had been due, not to any influence exerted by the Archbishop, but to the pressure of the disillusioned Prince of Wales and the resentful Duke of Buckingham—the latter ably supported by his chaplain and confessor, William Laud.

[1] D. H. Willson, *James I and VI* (1956), p. 446.

Buckingham had long since turned his back on his early patron, Abbot; Laud and Abbot were deeply antagonistic towards each other. The accession of the Prince of Wales to the throne was inevitably accompanied by the rise of Buckingham and Laud into positions of decisive influence in Church and State and the consequent depreciation of Abbot.

Apart from Abbot, there were in 1625 three other Churchmen who, either in virtue of the office they held or because of the personal influence they wielded, might have been regarded as candidates for royal favour. The first was Lancelot Andrewes, Bishop of Winchester. He had stood high in the favour of James I, but he never received the confidence of the new monarch in anything like the measure in which he had received that of his father. This was due partly to advanced age and partly to the fact that, whereas Charles was a man whose beliefs issued in strong action, Andrewes always appeared reluctant to impose conformity and discipline by force, however much he might exhort. Secondly, there was John Williams, but his days of grace were already numbered and after preaching King James's funeral sermon he was deprived of his office of Lord Keeper and ordered to withdraw to his diocese. The official reason for his relegation was on the ground of a technicality. The real reason was that Buckingham distrusted him and Charles found his laxity and worldliness intolerable.

That left William Laud. There were three reasons why Laud was more acceptable than Abbot to King Charles. In the first place, Charles was a young man who at the age of twenty-five looked for someone less aged, more active, and more determined than Abbot, who was sixty-three, old for his age through infirmity, and cautious in his handling of ecclesiastical affairs. Laud was fifty-two, in good health, full of vigour, a man of action and determination, who was already gaining a reputation as a disciplinarian. With such a Churchman already in royal favour, it was unlikely that the new King would look elsewhere for advice and leadership. Secondly, Charles was like his father in professing a profound belief in the Divine Right of Kings, but—unlike his father—he was prepared to act upon that belief. Abbot held no such exalted view of the nature of kingship and had already shown himself prepared, if need be, to resist the royal will. In

Laud, however, Charles had one who shared his belief and, like himself, was prepared to take the belief to its logical conclusion. Thirdly, there was the question of churchmanship. Both Laud and the King were of the Arminian school of theology. This represented an outlook standing half-way between Rome and Geneva and had been developed largely through the writings of Hooker and Andrewes. It rejected the Calvinist doctrine of predestination, emphasized the visible Church as a divine society, held a positive apologia for the Church of England based upon Scripture and the Fathers, maintained a high conception of episcopacy, and laid stress upon decency and order in public worship. Abbot was a Calvinist and thus rejected the main Arminian position, which in common with the great body of Puritans he regarded as subversive to the Reformation settlement. Moreover, the representatives of this "high Anglicanism" were concerned to enforce conformity and discipline and it was clear to Charles that Abbot, who favoured toleration, would be unwilling to enforce those things of which he disapproved. In the opinion of Charles, Laud was the one man able to guide the Church along what he believed to be the only correct path. In Laud the King had a bishop whose religious convictions were of a rock-like solidity, who was a man of prayer, who was utterly honest and incorruptible. Laud had a deep reverence for all the Church's ordered life, a contempt for covetousness, and a single-minded purposefulness. Unfortunately, these qualities were too often concealed behind an authoritarian temper, a harshness, and an asperity which earned him many enemies, gained him few friends, and brought about the temporary downfall of the Church of England.

The result of this combination of circumstances was that Abbot found himself out in the cold. Gradually he became Archbishop only in name, while the religious policy of Charles was practically dictated by Laud. Over all lay the net of Buckingham's influence. Charles did not approach the Archbishop for advice; Laud had his ear, and what Laud advised, the King instructed Abbot to put into operation. In fact the Archbishop came to be regarded as "little more than a nuisance, cumbering the ground which could have been more usefully occupied by a man of greater spiritual and mental stature",[1] and Laud hastened

---

[1] Paul A. Welsby, *Lancelot Andrewes*, p. 254.

to exclude him as far as possible from public life. His every move and word were seized upon by certain sections of the Court as an excuse for obloquy. Even his hospitality was a cause of criticism and suspicion. When King James had bestowed the archbishopric upon him he had charged him to "carry my House nobly (that was his Majesty's word) and live like an Archbishop; which I promised him to do: And when men came to my house, who were of civil sorts, I gave them friendly entertainment."[1] What irritated the Archbishop's critics was the sight of so many of their opponents resorting to Lambeth at dinner- and supper-time. Abbot was particularly hospitable to members of the High Commission and gave weekly entertainments for their benefit. In this too he was acting upon the late King's advice to him. Each month some of the bishops, divines, civilians, and judges were invited to dinner and Abbot later said that the number of guests on these occasions increased to such an extent that it became a burden. By 1627 he reckoned that it had cost him £1,500, "my house being like a great Hostry every Thursday, in Term; and for my Expenses, no man giving me so much as thanks".[2]

Another factor which contributed to Abbot's isolation and Laud's exaltation was that the Archbishop's increasing infirmity and disappointment gave him no encouragement to appear at Court or at the Council. Looking back in 1627 over the immediate years he wrote sadly: "I saw what little esteem was made of me and those things which belonged to mine own occupation; with Bishoprics and Deaneries, and other Church-places I was no more acquainted with than if I dwelt at Venice, and understood of them by some Gazette."[3]

It has already been seen how Abbot had been dropped from participation in the case of Richard Montague, whose theology was congenial to Charles and Laud and so repellent to Abbot. But it is significant that before he was excluded from this case Charles, at the very outset of his reign, had commanded Laud to go not to Abbot but to Bishop Andrewes, to "learn from him what he would have done in the cause of the Church, and bring back his answer, especially in the matter of his Five Articles".[4]

[1] "Archbishop Abbot his Narrative", in J. Rushworth, *Historical Collections* (1659), I, pp. 434 ff. [2] Ibid. [3] Ibid.
[4] W. Laud, "Diary", 9 April 1625, in *Works* (ed. W. Scott and J. Bliss,

Although it might be considered expedient to by-pass him on matters of fundamental ecclesiastical policy, the Archbishop could safely be permitted to execute routine matters. Thus on 24 June after the plague had been raging in London for several months, Abbot and certain other bishops were instructed by the King to advise about a public fast and form of prayer, "to implore the divine mercy, now that the pestilence began to spread, and the extraordinary wet weather threatened a famine; and also to beg the divine blessing upon the fleet ready to put to sea". After a meeting for this purpose Abbot and the other bishops waited upon the new Queen and kissed her hand.[1] The action of the King in seeking advice about a fast would appear to have been the result of a petition from Parliament, for on the previous day Abbot had been on a committee of the Lords to confer with the Commons about the latter's proposal that a petition be made to the King to appoint a general fast.[2] The life of this first Parliament of the new reign was short and Abbot was absent from nearly half the sittings because of ill health.

The New Year (1626) saw the abatement of the plague and 29 January was observed as a day of thanksgiving when a Form of Prayer was used which had been drawn up by Abbot and five other bishops.[3] Four days later, on the Feast of the Purification, Charles I was crowned in Westminster Abbey. The King had desired that a special revision of the Coronation service should be made and he had issued a Commission for this purpose to Abbot and other bishops, among whom the most energetic was Laud, whose notes show the minute care with which he prepared every detail. The resulting service, based on ancient sources, has not since been substantially altered. Williams was in disgrace and was forbidden by the King to officiate as Dean of Westminster, and Laud was appointed to act as his deputy. Consequently the greater part of the preparations within the Abbey were entirely in his hands and to him fell the task of reminding the King to

---

1847–60), III, p. 160. The Five Articles were directions concerning certain ceremonies which James I had proposed to impose upon the Church in Scotland.

[1] W. Laud, "Diary", 24 June 1625, in *Works,* III, p. 165.
[2] *Journals of the House of Lords,* III, 23 June 1625.
[3] W. Laud, "Diary", 18 Jan. 1626, in *Works,* III, p. 166.

spend the eve of his Coronation in prayer and meditation. Archbishop Abbot, however, as his office demanded, officiated at the service and crowned the King.[1]

Soon afterwards, on Passion Sunday, Godfrey Goodman, Bishop of Gloucester, preached before the King a sermon which led to the accusation of popery. He had emphasized the doctrine of the Real Presence and was questioned "for preaching transubstantiation, or near it before the King".[2] Charles commanded Archbishop Abbot, together with Neile of Durham, Andrewes of Winchester, and Laud, to consult together about the sermon. There can be no doubt that Abbot found Goodman's views uncongenial, but he carried little sway against the other bishops whom Charles had appointed as his colleagues, all of whom were of Arminian tendencies. After the meeting they advised the King "that nothing was innovated by him in the doctrine of the Church of England. That the best way would be that the Bishop should preach the sermon again, at some time chosen by himself, and should then show them how and wherein he was misunderstood."[3] The very mildness of the admonition represented another triumph for Laud, and Goodman, although he agreed to do what was suggested, gave little satisfaction to his critics.

The Coronation had been followed by the summoning of Parliament. Abbot's ill health kept him from attending the early sittings. At the beginning of March he put in appearances on eight days, being carried into the House and permitted to speak sitting.[4] For the rest of the month and for the whole of April he was again absent through sickness. He returned on 1 May, the day upon which charges were opened against the Earl of Bristol, who was accused of high treason on the instigation of Charles I in order to prevent him revealing what had actually occurred during the visit of the Prince and Buckingham to Madrid in

[1] J. Rushworth, *Historical Collections*, I, p. 202 f; cf. *The Manner of the Coronation of King Charles I* (ed. C. Wordsworth, 1892).

[2] Revd J. Mead to Sir Martin Stuteville, 15 April 1626—T. Birch, *Court and Times of Charles I* (1848), I, p. 95. Cf. Geoffrey Soden, *Godfrey Goodman, Bishop of Gloucester, 1583–1656* (1953), pp. 159 ff.

[3] W. Laud, "Diary", 12 April 1626, in *Works*, III, p. 187.

[4] *Notes on Debates in the House of Lords, 1624 and 1626* (ed. S. R. Gardiner, 1879), p. 148.

1623.[1] Abbot was a member of the committee appointed by the Lords "to take Examinations of the Proofs and Witnesses concerning the King's charge against the Earl".[2] As a result of Bristol's damaging revelations, the Commons drew up an impeachment of the Duke of Buckingham, and Charles, rather than risk the chance of its success, decided on 15 June to dissolve Parliament. Abbot was on the committee of the Lords which on that day drew up a petition moving his Majesty to continue Parliament, but the effort was abortive.[3]

The purpose of summoning Parliament had been the alarming state of the nation's finances. The government was virtually bankrupt, there were heavy loans outstanding, an attempt to pawn the crown jewels in Amsterdam had failed, and a promise had been made to pay £30,000 to the King of Denmark for his support against the Catholic League in Germany. The Commons had refused to grant supply unless Buckingham was dismissed. Now that Parliament was dissolved and no money had been forthcoming, the King's financial plight was desperate, particularly in view of the fact that the country, already at war with Spain, appeared to be drifting into war with France. There were many discussions in Council "to find suitable remedies", but Abbot, although he gave private advice, did not attend because of his ill health and the strained relationship between him and Buckingham.[4] Charles first tried to raise money by a benevolence, but when that proved a failure he determined to try a Forced Loan. The resistance throughout the country was obstinate and intense, the judges refused to acknowledge the legality of the Loan, and a number of defaulters were imprisoned. Abbot was not present in Council when the Loan was decided upon, but it is certain that he did not approve. He recognized the King's need for money, but he also remembered that Parliament had been prepared to grant him considerable sums in return for redress of grievances, and "it ran in my mind that the old and usual was best—that it was sweeter when the Prince and the People tuned well together".[5]

[1] *Journals of the House of Lords*, III, 1 May 1626.
[2] Ibid., 22 May.   [3] Ibid., 15 June 1626.
[4] Venetian Ambassador to the Doge and Senate, 27 Nov. 1626—*S.P. Venetian*, xix, no. 49.
[5] "Archbishop Abbot his Narrative", in J. Rushworth, *Historical Collections*, I, pp. 434 ff.

At the opening of the Commission for the Loan Abbot was sent for, but he said nothing, "for the confusion was such that I knew not what to make of it".[1]

In the midst of these critical events Dr Robert Sibthorpe mounted the pulpit of the Church of St Sepulchre, Northampton, to preach the Assize Sermon on 22 February 1627. He thus attained a nation-wide notoriety, for in the course of his discourse he asserted that "the Prince, who is the head, and makes his Court and Council, it is his duty to direct and make laws. Eccles. 8.3 and 4, He doth whatsoever pleases him. Where the word of the King is, there is power, and who may say to him, What doest thou? . . . If princes command anything which subjects may not perform, because it is against the laws of God, or of nature, or impossible: Yet subjects are bound to undergo the punishment, without either resisting, or railing, or reviling, and so to yield a passive obedience where they cannot exhibit an active one."[2] He went on to justify the King's proceedings in levying a Forced Loan and the subject's necessary obedience as a religious duty, asserting that the sovereign is absolute master of the property of his subjects, that he might dispose of it at will, and that for conscience sake the subjects must acquiesce and obey.

A copy of this sermon was sent to the Duke of Buckingham who immediately saw in it an invaluable piece of propaganda for the King's cause. It was accordingly forwarded to Abbot for the latter's licence to publish.[3] The Archbishop's health was poor and for some time he had been absent from Court. He was so crippled with gout that he found it impossible to stand or walk without assistance and he was also troubled with "the Stone". This physical incapacity was sufficient of itself to keep him from Court and Council, but he himself admitted that, in addition, the state of political affairs had "no great invitements to draw me abroad".

[1] Ibid.

[2] Robert Sibthorpe, *Of Apostolic Obedience. Showing the Duty of Subjects to pay Tribute and Taxes to their Parishes, according to the Word of God, in the Law and the Gospel* . . . (Published 1627).

[3] For Abbot's connection with the Sibthorpe affair and his subsequent sequestration, we are dependent upon "Archbishop Abbot his Narrative", written in his own hand and printed in J. Rushworth, *Historical Collections*, I, pp. 434 ff; W. Cobbett, *Complete Collection of State Trials* (1809), II, pp. 1451 ff.

He was thus content to live in semi-retirement and to possess his soul in patience "till God sent fairer weather". Now there came upon him, once again, a crisis in his fortunes which his conscience would not permit him to avert.

The King sent to Abbot a message by William Murry of the Royal Bedchamber requiring him to license Sibthorpe's sermon and requesting him to read it personally. He agreed to read it and promised to express his opinion on it in a day or two. It soon became clear to him that it was a dangerous sermon, not least to the King himself. When Murry returned for the Archbishop's answer, Abbot told him that the sermon seemed to him to be dangerous, inaccurate, and inflammatory, and begged him to acquaint the King with the fact. Two or three days later Murry again called on Abbot with the King's reply, which failed to satisfy the Archbishop. As he was too lame to wait on the King personally he requested that his Majesty would send to him the Bishop of Bath and Wells (Laud) to whom he would make known his scruples. Murry was back again a few days later with the message that the King "did not think it fit to send the Bishop of *Bath* unto me; but he expected that I should pass the Book". The Duke of Buckingham now took a hand and urged the King to expedite the matter. Once again William Murry waited on the Archbishop and this time his communication from the King was threatening—"That if I did not dispatch it, the King would take some other course with me." Abbot then put his objections in writing and sent them to Charles. They were answered by Laud, whom Abbot described as "the only inward Counsellor with Buckingham, sitting with him sometimes privately whole hours, and feeding his humour with malice and pride".

When Murry brought this answer, he found Abbot "ill in a Sweat by a fit of the Stone" and did not stay. Abbot retired to bed and, after a night sleepless with pain, received Murry at his bedside. Abbot was subjected to the indignity of a refusal to be permitted to read Laud's reply himself, for Murry had had instructions not to allow the paper to pass out of his hands but to read its contents aloud to the Archbishop. When he had heard the reply, Abbot remained quite unconvinced by it and declared that, unless he was given the opportunity of examining the question more closely and thoroughly, he could not license the sermon. He later commented:

> If I had been in Council, when the Project of the Loan was first handled, I would have used my best reasons to have it well-grounded, but I was absent. . . . And since it was brought into execution, I did not interpose myself to know the grounds of it. It seemed therefore strange to me, that in the upshot of the business I was called upon to make good by Divinity, which others had done; and must have no other inducement to it but Dr Sibthorpe's contemptible Treatise.

He likened the situation to the one in which he found himself at the time of the Essex Divorce, for in each case a course of action had been decided upon by others for their own reasons, but the Archbishop had to be brought in to cloak the decision in judicial or theological decency.

When it was clear that Abbot was not to be moved, the sermon was licensed by the Bishop of London after it had been revised in the light of some of Abbot's objections. At the same time it was decided that Abbot should suffer. When his friends reported this to him he withdrew to Croydon a month before his usual time. The next move occurred on Tuesday 5 July when Lord Conway journeyed from Oatlands to Croydon bearing the King's order that Abbot was to withdraw to Canterbury. Abbot was very unwilling to retire to his metropolitical city because of his disagreements with the citizens. "If I should be among them, I have many adversaries of the citizens. . . . I would be unwilling that my servants and the people should fall together by the ears, while I am in the Town." If the King would permit it, he proposed to go instead to his house at Ford, five miles beyond Canterbury. Conway promised to consult with the King. For a few days after Conway had left Abbot heard no news and so he wrote to Conway about his proposed place of residence, and to this letter he had reply that the King permitted him to withdraw to Ford.

Abbot felt his position acutely. He wrote of the strangeness of

> that, which by way of Censure was inflicted upon me, being then of the age of Sixty five years, incumbered with the Gout, and afflicted with the Stone, having lived so many years in a

place of great Service. . . . Yet this Innocency and good Fame to be overturned in a month, and a Christian Bishop suddenly to be made *Fabula Vulgi*, to be tossed upon the Tongues of Friends and Foes, of Protestants and Papists, of Court and County, of English and Foreignors, must needs in common opinion presuppose some Crime, open or secret.

Even at Ford this pathetic figure was not left unmolested. He encountered the King's displeasure by conferring the Vicarage of Lydd upon the Dean of Canterbury. In a letter to King Charles he maintained that he had acted on the advice of learned counsel "for the safety of my charge and preservation of the patronage of the Archbishops in succession . . . whose rights and liberties I am bound by oath to maintain".[1] Moreover, he was receiving misrepresentation at Court, where it had been given out that if the Dean of Canterbury resigned his benefice to the King the Archbishop would not permit the King to use it but would bestow it upon one of his own chaplains. This, wrote Abbot, "I do absolutely deny".[2] There can be no doubt that Abbot felt acutely his isolation from the centre of affairs. "Being here out of the way, I understand not how my own business faireth at London or the Court."[3]

His business was in fact faring very badly, for the previous day his jurisdiction had been put in commission, to be exercised by the Bishops of London, Durham, Rochester, Oxford, and Bath and Wells,[4] and "it was said that when the other bishops hesitated to sign the order for his suspension, Laud, though the junior of them all, demanded the pen and placed his signature first".[5] It is interesting to notice the names of these bishops to whom the archiepiscopal jurisdiction had been committed. Peter Heylyn pointed out that they were "no Favourers of that [i.e. the Puritan] Faction" and that Charles's purpose, now Abbot was

---

[1] Abbot to the King, 10 Oct. 1627—Cowper MSS. (*Hist. MSS. Comm. Reports,* Series 23 (I), pp. 326 f).

[2] Ibid.

[3] Abbot to Sir John Coke, 10 Oct. 1627—Cowper MSS. (op. cit., p. 327).

[4] 9 Oct. 1627—*S.P. Dom. Chas. I.* lxxx, 72; D. Wilkins, *Concilia Magnae Britanniae et Hiberniae* (1731), IV, p. 174; J. Rushworth, *Historical Collections,* I, pp. 431 ff.

[5] H. Trevor-Roper, *Archbishop Laud* (1940), p. 80.

out of the way, was that "some stop might be given to that current which then began to bear all before it".[1]

Sequestration was such a drastic punishment for the action which led to it that it is tempting to see behind it motives other than displeasure at the refusal to license Sibthorpe's sermon. "The Church", wrote Peter Heylyn, " . . . was at that time in a heavy condition, and opportunities must be watched for keeping her from falling from bad to worse." The increase in conventicles, Puritanism, etc. was

> a pregnant evidence, that possibly there could not be a greater mischief in the Church of God than a Popular Prelate. . . . There was no need to tell [the King] from what fountain the mischief came, how much the Popularity and remiss Government of *Abbot* did contribute towards it. Him therefore he sequestered from his *Metropolitical* Jurisdiction, confines him to his house at *Ford* in *Kent*.[2]

When allowance has been made for Heylyn's bias against the Archbishop, there may be considerable truth in what he said, especially when the shadow of William Laud can be seen looming in the background throughout the proceedings. Abbot himself was certain that his misfortunes were due to his enemies and he maintained that his absence from Court through ill health "gave occasion to Maligners to traduce me".[3]

There were a few who said that he was sequestered "on the old account of that homicide",[4] and it may well be that the fresh cause of offence renewed "his former obnoxiousness for that casualty".[5] Thomas Fuller evidently thought this opinion was held strongly enough for him to list eight reasons why, at the time, the proceedings taken against Abbot in 1627 were "generally considered as over-rigid and severe" if they had been taken on account of the old homicide.[6] Fuller himself held the opinion

---

[1] P. Heylyn, *Cyprianus Anglicus*, p. 169.

[2] Ibid.

[3] "Archbishop Abbot his Narrative", in J. Rushworth, *Historical Collections*, I.

[4] T. Fuller, *The Worthies of England* (ed. J. Freeman, 1952), p. 552; *Church History of Britain* (1655), Bk. xi, sec. 1, par. 51.

[5] T. Fuller, *The Worthies of England*, p. 552.

[6] T. Fuller, *Church History of Britain*, Bk. xi, sec. 1, par. 51.

that "the Archbishop's own stiffness and averseness to comply with the Court-Designs, advantaged his Adversaries against him, and made him more obnoxious to the King's displeasure".[1] He also put his finger on another most potent cause of Abbot's disgrace. "The blame did most light on *Bishop Laud*, men accounting this a kind of *Filius ante diem,* etc. As if not content to *succeed,* he endeavoured to *supplant* him; who might well have suffered his decayed old age to have died in honour."[2] It is of significance that in the Commission of Sequestration there is no express mention of the Sibthorpe Sermon, but only the general remark that "the said archbishop could not at that present, in his own person, attend those services which were otherwise proper for his cognizance and jurisdiction".

Thomas Fuller maintained that two benefits accrued to Abbot as a result of his sequestration. In the first place, he became "beloved of Men"—not so much on personal grounds, but because "the *Country* hath constantly a *blessing* for those, for whom the *Court* hath a *curse*". Secondly, "he may charitably be presumed to love God the more, whose service he did the better attend, being freed from the drudgery of the world, as that soul which hath the *least* of *Martha* hath the *most* of *Mary* therein".[3]

[1] Ibid.   [2] Ibid.
[3] *Church History of Britain,* Bk. xi, sec. 1, par. 53.

10

"Restored unto his Jurisdiction"

As we grow older
The world becomes stranger, the pattern more complicated
Of dead and living.

. . . . . .

Old men ought to be explorers
Here and there does not matter
We must be still and still moving
Into another intensity
For a further union, a deeper communion
Through the dark cold and the empty desolation
. . . In my end is my beginning.

T. S. ELIOT, *East Coker*

THE YEAR 1628 opened with Abbot still in enforced retirement and with his jurisdiction continuing to be exercised by commission. On 7 January the King issued a warrant renewing the High Commission and inserting therein the Archbishop of Canterbury,[1] but it seems unlikely that Charles expected him to take his seat on that body, for in February the Attorney-General asked Secretary Conway to remind the King to recommend a fit person to be Abbot's deputy in Convocation.[2] Abbot received his summons to Parliament and Convocation, but the King wrote him a letter instructing him to attend neither. Shortly afterwards there was a proclamation "requiring all men interested in Parliament to be there on the day appointed". This caused Abbot to write to Lord Keeper Coventry that "if the

[1] The King to Attorney-General Heath, 7 Jan. 1628—*S.P. Dom. Chas. I*, xc, 29.

[2] Attorney-General Heath to Secretary Conway, 24 Feb. 1628—ibid., xciv. 35.

King be graciously pleased to take off his restraint", he would be
ready in those two assemblies "to perform his duty to God and his
Church, to the King and kingdom".[1] Coventry forwarded the
letter to Secretary Conway in order to discover the royal pleasure.
The King remained immovable and directed Abbot to send his
proxy both to Parliament and to Convocation. The choice of proxy
in Parliament was left to Abbot, but he was ordered by the King
to send the Bishop of Bath and Wells (Laud) as his proxy to
Convocation.[2]

Parliament itself then took a hand. As soon as it met the House
of Lords requested the King that Abbot, the Bishop of Lincoln,
and the Earl of Bristol, all of whom had been forbidden by the
King to take their seats, should be permitted to attend the House.
The King granted the request and there were those who said that
he had ordered them to absent themselves merely "in order to
mollify Parliament by this first act of grace".[3]

By his coercive measures Charles had managed to raise a sub-
stantial sum of money, but it was in no way commensurate with
the pressing needs of the government. It was for this reason that
he had recourse again to Parliament, the third and most fatal of
his reign. The Commons proved to be quite unmanageable and
insisted upon voicing their grievances before voting supplies.
They drew up a protest against arbitrary imprisonment, forced
loans, and the billeting of soldiers, and incorporated it into a Petition of Right. When the matter came before the Lords it was the
occasion for a notable debate on whether the King or Council
may arbitrarily imprison. Abbot pointed out in his speech that
the King was the fountain of honour and justice, although some
had impudently published that kings were not bound to do justice.
He cited several passages from Scripture to prove that princes
ought to do justice, and his conclusion was that imprisonment
was "so great that a cause is to be shown for it". He added that
he had been prompted to say this "in discharge of his conscience,
and reputes it a great blessing of God on the King and on us that

[1] Abbot to Lord Keeper Coventry, 26 Feb. 1628—*S.P. Dom. Chas. I*,
xciv, 83 (i).
[2] Secretary Conway to Abbot, 3 March 1628—*S.P. Dom. Chas. I*, xcv, 14.
[3] Venetian Ambassador to the Doge and Senate, 5 April 1628—*S.P.
Venetian*, xxi, no. 58; *Journals of the House of Lords*, III.

we may dispute thus".[1] For ten hours the debate continued and "the decisive impulse came at last from Abbot who pointed out the ruinous consequences of a breach with the Lower House in the face of so many enemies abroad".[2] It was agreed that instead of accepting or rejecting the Commons' resolutions the Lords should draw up counter-proposals. A month later the Houses had still failed to agree and Abbot advised the Lords to "join with the Commons in the petition, though he would have had also some demonstration of their saving of the King's just prerogative".[3]

The Commons attacked Roger Manwaring and Robert Sibthorpe for their propagandist sermons in support of the government. Manwaring had preached two sermons before the King in July 1627 in which he had asserted, like Sibthorpe earlier, the duty of subjects to pay taxes demanded by kings, "if upon necessity extreme and urgent", and he had declared that it would be hard for a subject "to defend his conscience from that heavy prejudice of resisting the ordinance of God, and receiving to himself damnation".[4] The sermons were severely attacked in the Commons in March 1628, and on 9 June Manwaring was impeached before the Lords. He appeared at the Bar of the House of Lords to answer the charge of the Commons against him. After his speech of defence, during which the Lords interrupted him several times, he wished to withdraw, but he was recalled by Abbot who admonished him severely. The "Participation which Dr Mainwaring gave to the King with God" the Archbishop regarded as "very Blasphemy". His assertion that justice appertained only to equals and that thus there was none between God and man nor between the King and his people was impious and false. In fact "the Scriptures do plainly declare and prove a Justice from God to Man . . . and from the King to his People. And further, That, by the Laws of God and Man, there was ever a communitive Justice for Government." Abbot then reminded

[1] 22 April 1628—*Notes on Debates in the House of Lords, 1621, 1625, 1628* (ed. F. H. Relf, 1929), p. 127.

[2] S. R. Gardiner, *History of England, 1603–42* (1883–4), VI, p. 258.

[3] "Minute Book"—House of Lords MSS., quoted S. R. Gardiner, op. cit., VI, p. 289.

[4] *Religion and Allegiance: in two Sermons, preached before the King's Majesty* . . . (1627).

him of the philosopher Anacharsis, "whom the King of Cyprus caused to be brayed in Brasen Mortar, for his base Flattery (a just reward for all flatterers of Princes)".[1] Manwaring was sentenced to a fine of £1,000, to imprisonment during the pleasure of the House, and to be suspended from preaching anywhere for three years and before the Court for ever.

Two days before, the Commons had drawn up a Remonstrance calling for the strict enforcement of the penal laws and the suppression of Arminianism. Then they turned their attention to Buckingham and demanded his dismissal from all offices. Once again, in order to save his minister, the King prorogued Parliament. During the recess Laud was translated from Bath and Wells to the influential See of London, and Buckingham was murdered. Of the latter event Hugh Trevor-Roper has written:

> Rarely has a political assassination been hailed with more universal delight. It was not only greeted with enthusiasm by those whose indignation and hatred were aroused against the omnipotent and omnicompetent minister: it brought relief to those who were conscientiously seeking some way out of the impasse into which the affairs of the Kingdom had been brought by the King's refusal to sacrifice either the favourite or the policy he embodied.[2]

It might be thought that the assassination brought relief to Abbot, but in fact the Duke's disappearance from the scene had little effect upon him, for he still had Laud to contend with and Buckingham's death did Laud more harm than good. "The death of Buckingham enabled the government to drop Buckingham's foreign policy, and the peace which followed allowed Laud leisure, and freedom from parliamentary influence, in which to realise, or attempt to realise, the programme in which he was really interested."[3]

Although Buckingham's death in no way lessened the power of Laud, other factors were working in Abbot's favour. Charles still desperately needed the co-operation of Parliament in order to solve his financial problems. In response to the Commons'

---

[1] *Journals of the House of Lords*, III—13 June 1628.
[2] H. Trevor-Roper, *Archbishop Laud* (1940), p. 87.
[3] Ibid.

Remonstrance urging the suppression of Arminian doctrine he issued a Declaration, recommended by Laud and approved by the other bishops, forbidding dogmatic discussion, and prefixed to a new edition of the Articles of Religion. "The next step was to obtain assent of both parties among the bishops. Montague was induced to write a letter to Abbot in which he disclaimed any wish to uphold Arminianism. Abbot accepted the hand thus held out to him."[1] On 11 December he appeared once more at White-hall, kissed the King's hand, was bidden to attend the meetings of the Council, and "was restored unto his Jurisdiction".[2] "The Archbishop of Canterbury has been restored to favour," wrote the Venetian Ambassador, "and is a follower of the right party."[3]

In spite of Charles's Declaration enjoining peace and unity in the Church, Parliament reassembled in January 1629 in a turbulent mood. Abbot was absent for the greater part of the session, which witnessed the Commons' truculent attack upon the religious policy of the government and upon Bishop Neile, Bishop Montague, and John Cosin, and which ended amid scenes of confusion on 2 March, the Speaker being held firmly in his chair. After this violent expression of opinion in Parliament the King was convinced that preachers were adding fuel to the flames by seditiously proclaiming that "religion doth totter, and that the purity of the Gospel is in great hazard". He asked Abbot and the other bishops in London to consider the whole question. Abbot addressed a letter to one of his bishops in which he informed him that it was the King's command that within his diocese he was in his own person "to preach obedience to the highest magistrate as to the Lieutenant of God ... and that you cause the ministry of your diocese to forbear all undutiful speech in the pulpit as if there were like to be any innovation or alteration in religion, which, we thank God and our own gracious Sovereign, is not to be feared".[4]

In spite of his restoration to favour Abbot was still eclipsed by

---

[1] S. R. Gardiner, *History of England, 1603–42* (1883–4), VII, p. 21.

[2] P. Heylyn, *Cyprianus Anglicus,* p. 169.

[3] Venetian Ambassador to the Venetian Ambassador in France, 29 Dec. 1628—*S.P. Venetian,* xxi, no. 656.

[4] Abbot to one of the bishops in his own province, April 1629—*S.P. Dom. Chas. I,* cxl, 37.

The Hospital of the
Blessed Trinity, Guildford

Archbishop Abbot's Monument

Laud. He was old, he was infirm, every movement he made to oppose the rising tide of Arminianism was fruitless, and he now lived partly in retirement, either at his hospital at Guildford, at his house at Ford, at Croydon, or at Lambeth, where he was reported to turn midnight into noonday, receiving nocturnal visits of "all the malcontents in Church and State".[1] Although he possessed the office of authority, the source of authority had passed to Laud. One of the clearest manifestations of this was in the issue of instructions to the bishops in December 1629. These instructions were drawn up by Laud and the King ordered Abbot to send them out. "These instructions aimed at increasing the efficiency of the bishops by keeping them, sufficiently provided, in their dioceses, where they were to exercise themselves husbanding the attenuated resources of the Church and disorganizing the Puritan Ministry."[2] To this end the bishops were ordered to reside in their Sees in one of their episcopal houses, to hold ordinations with solemnity, to have a special vigilance over lecturers and private chaplains, to refrain from making leases, and to give an annual account of their "performance of these our commands".[3] As soon as these instructions reached him, Abbot circulated them to the bishops in his province. Heylyn suggested that the Archbishop regarded them as "being looked on as an Artifice to bring in Arminianism", and that he was particularly displeased with the limitations which were laid on Lecturers.[4] Indeed, he appears to have restored to their lectureships two men in his own diocese who had been suspended by the Dean and Archdeacon of Canterbury.[5] On the other hand he approved of the order to the bishops to reside in their dioceses. "Praise God", he wrote to Secretary Dorchester, "for the King's care for the residence of Bishops and others."[6]

There is little evidence of Abbot taking part in public affairs during 1630. He was too infirm to baptize the infant Prince Charles

---

[1] "Archbishop Abbot his Narrative", in J. Rushworth, *Historical Collections*, I.

[2] H. Trevor-Roper, *Archbishop Laud* (1940), pp. 104 f.

[3] Lambeth MSS., 943, f. 103; W. Laud, *Works*, V, p. 307.

[4] Peter Heylyn, *Cyprianus Anglicus*, p. 201.

[5] Ibid.

[6] Abbot to Secretary Dorchester, 22 Oct. 1630—*S.P. Dom. Chas. I*, clxxiv, 70.

at St James's in June. That was another honour which passed to Laud,[1] although Abbot had some interest in the ceremony for he wrote to the Dean of Canterbury about a silver font which had formerly been used for royal christenings and which he had heard had been deposited with the Dean and Chapter of Canterbury. He requested the Dean to search for it and to send it up to London in safety.[2] In October he was worried about securing a sufficient number of bishops to consecrate the new Bishop of Peterborough (William Piers). This was due partly to the plague that was once again rampant, and partly to the effect of the King's instructions that bishops should reside in their dioceses. Both facts made it difficult to get bishops to London. Abbot had to postpone the consecration and to send messages to each bishop to require him on his oath of canonical obedience to assist at the service.[3] In the end the Bishops of Winchester and Oxford took part, as did also the Bishop of Rochester, who had to be sent for from Rochester, and the Bishop of St David's, who was already in London on business.[4]

In January 1631 a certain William Page took up his pen and began to write a reply to a book[5] by William Prynne, in which the latter had fiercely attacked the practice of bowing in church. Abbot ordered Page, on the authority of the Royal Declaration,[6] to desist from disputation. "Good Mr Page," wrote Abbot's Secretary, "my Lord of Canterbury is informed that you are publishing a treatise touching the question of bowing at the name of Jesus, an argument wherein Mr Widdowes foolishly,[7] and Mr Prynne scurrilously, have already, to the scandal of the Church, exercised their pens." To persist in arguing the question would be to foment "bitterness and intestine contestations". But once again Abbot was thwarted by Laud, who encouraged Page to ignore the Archbishop and to continue his work.[8]

[1] W. Laud, "Diary", 27 June 1630, in *Works*, III, p. 212.

[2] Abbot to the Dean of Canterbury, 20 June 1630—*Archaeologia Cantiana*, Vol. 42 (1930), p. 105.

[3] Abbot to Secretary Dorchester, 22 Oct. 1630—*S.P. Dom. Chas. I*, clxxiv, 70.   [4] Same to same, 28 Oct. 1630—ibid., 96.

[5] *Lame Giles, His Haltings* (1630).   [6] See above, p. 136.

[7] *The Lawless Kneelingless Schismatical Puritan* (1630).

[8] W. Laud, *Works*, V, pp. 39 ff. Page's book was published in 1631, under the title *A Treatise or justification of bowing at the name of Jesus* . . .

Abbot was in constant attendance on the High Commission in 1631 and 1632, but, although the surviving records show him almost as enthusiastic as Laud in his enforcement of conformity, here again the last word was most often with Laud. When Samuel Pretty, a Puritan minister, was brought before the Commission, "the Archbishop then would only have imprisoned and suspended him from his ministerial office, but it was moved by the Bishop of London [Laud] that he might undergo the Censure of the Court, and that to be given in order, for that he and others were minded to degrade him", and Laud's view prevailed.[1] William Slater, a Doctor of Divinity who had added to the Psalms "a scandalous table to the disgrace of religion", was dismissed after receiving a reproof from Abbot, but Laud recalled him and lectured him severely on the cut of his clothes.[2] As an example of Abbot's manner on the High Commission, the following may be cited from the case of a number of Puritans charged on 3 May 1632 with holding a conventicle at Black-friars:

> You show yourselves most unthankful to God, to the King, and to the Church of England, that when (God be praised) through his Majesty's care and ours you have preaching in every church, and men have liberty to join in prayer and participation of the Sacraments and have catechisings and all to enlighten you, and which may serve you in the way of salvation; you in an unthankful manner cast off all this yoke, and in private unlawfully assemble yourselves together, making rents and divisions in the Church. If anything be amiss, let it be known, if anything be not agreeable to the word of God, we shall be as ready to redress it as you, but whereas it is nothing but your own imaginations, and you are unlearned men that seek to make up a religion of your own hands, I doubt no persuasion will serve the turn. We must take this course: you are called here: let them stand upon their bonds, and let us see what they will answer, it may be they will answer what may please us.[3]

[1] *Reports of Cases in the Courts of Star Chamber and High Commission* (ed. S. R. Gardiner, 1886), pp. 181 ff.
[2] Ibid., p. 186.   [3] Ibid., p. 280.

At the next sitting of the Court, however, Abbot took little part in the proceedings and Laud dealt with most of the cases. A minor point of interest which emerges from these reports is Abbot's dislike of the term "Roman Catholic". On two occasions he maintained that it was an absurd phrase, implying a contradiction. "Rome is a particular Church, Catholic is universal, then this is as much as to say of a particular universal Church; Nonsense!"[1] The one case affecting ceremonial among the surviving records of the Court shows that Abbot was by no means indifferent to due order in worship. Some parishioners claimed the right to seats above the Communion Table in the Church of St Austin, London. Abbot declared his dislike of the arrangement and ordered those parishioners to submit to their Ordinary—i.e. Laud![2]

It will be recalled that when the King issued his Instructions to the bishops, the latter were required to make a report once a year on how the instructions were being performed. It is not known whether Abbot did so in 1631, but his report of 2 January 1632 is extant. In it he noted that, "for aught it appeared", the bishops had resided at home and in their episcopal houses, except the Bishop of St David's who had remained in London on account of his wife's illness and because of a lawsuit in which he was engaged. "On Arminian points there is no dispute: and ordination of ministers, for aught that I can learn, are canonically observed: the rules for lecturers are strictly kept." Divine service had been read carefully and had been attended by the parishioners, except for certain separatists about London. There were very few non-conforming ministers in the Church. "There being nothing more, it may be the great comfort of your majesty, that in so large and diffuse a multitude both of men and matters, upon strict examination, there is so little exorbitancy to be found."[3] The whole report bears an aura of indifference, and the repeated phrases, "for aught it appeareth", "for aught I could learn", indicate a lack of real interest.

In July the King wrote to Abbot and instructed him to inform his suffragans that they were not to admit any incumbent until inquiry had been made whether the benefice in question was in

[1] Ibid., p. 300; cf. p. 195.
[2] Ibid., p. 309.   [3] Lambeth MSS., 943, f. 105.

the King's gift. The reason for this was that a number of benefices which of right belonged to the King had been presented to by private persons. Enclosed with the King's letter was a minute, with alterations in Laud's handwriting, thus revealing the true source of the instructions.[1] Later in the month further orders were issued to the Archbishop according to which he was to return by 10 October a certificate stating which benefices once in the patronage of the Crown had since Queen Elizabeth's reign been presented to by other persons.[2] All this is further evidence that Abbot's position was such that although he was Archbishop he directed nothing, but was rather the machine which put into operation the directions of others.

Laud's elevation to the Primacy appeared imminent in the summer of 1632 when Abbot became gravely ill with gout. He made a good recovery, however, and in September a letter-writer reported that

> His Grace by his diet hath so moderated his gout as it is now rather an infirmity than a pain. He looks fresh and enjoys his health, and hath his wits and intellectuals about him; so that if any other prelate do gape after his benefice, His Grace perhaps (according to that old and homely proverb) may eat of the goose which shall graze upon his grave.[3]

The same letter gives a delightful description of a meeting between the Earl of Arundel and the old Archbishop, to whose safe care the Earl's son, Lord Maltravers, had been committed when he had offended King Charles.

> One day last week my Lord of Arundel and his son, my Lord Maltravers, having espied my Lord of Canterbury's coach on Banstead Downs coming towards theirs, before they came a butt's length short of it, both their lordships alighted, and went a great pace towards his grace's coach; who, when they approached, said, "What! and must my lord marshal of England take so great pains to do me so much honour? Were my legs as good as my heart, I should have met your lordships the

[1] The King to Abbot, 8 July 1632—*S.P. Dom. Chas. I*, ccxx, 36.
[2] Same to same, 17 July 1632—ibid., 79.
[3] Mr Pory to Sir Thomas Puckering, 20 Sept. 1632—T. Birch, *Court and Times of Charles I* (1848), II, p. 177.

better half of the way." Then my Lord of Arundel replied, "It might well become an earl marshal to give so much respect to an Archbishop of Canterbury, besides the peculiar obligation from his lordship to his grace for his noble usage of his sons and daughter Maltravers, while they were his prisoners." Whereupon my lord's grace took occasion to congratulate unto both my Lord Maltravers' brave and hopeful progeny of three sons and a daughter; and so they parted.[1]

David Mathew showed perception when he wrote of this incident.

The air of the Jacobean world, with its ease and its heavy cheerfulness, is brought back in the very turn and structure of these sentences. . . . This was how England had been ruled, the great bland ease at the coach window. It was in the tradition of Queen Elizabeth; it had nothing in common with Charles I.[2]

During these last years of his life Abbot continued to watch actively over the interests of All Souls College. He was still concerned that the surplus income should be well used and not be extravagantly spent by the Fellows, but in 1629 he allowed "for this time . . . a double livery", although he made the strong recommendation for the future that "when such money cometh extraordinarily unto you it be employed in buying of books and furnishing of your studies, and not spent upon vanities which carry nothing with them but distemper and disorder".[3] He still remained unsuccessful in enforcing discipline, for, although he had remarked triumphantly in 1628 that he had "quelled the faction which was wont to disquiet your college",[4] at the end of 1632 he was pained beyond endurance by the rioting that took place at Christmas. He wrote to the college in January 1633:

The Feast of Christmas drawing to an end doth put me in mind of the great outrage which, I am informed, was the last year committed in your college, where, although matters had formerly been carried with distemper, yet men did never break forth into that intolerable liberty as to tear off the doors and

[1] Ibid.   [2] David Mathew, *The Age of Charles I* (1951), p. 105.
[3] M. Burrows, *Worthies of All Souls* (1874), p. 112.
[4] Ibid., p. 133.

gates which are the fences of the College, and so to disquiet their neighbours as if it had been in a camp or town of war, to the great disgrace of the government of that University.

He then pointed a strange and solemn warning. More people had died in All Souls in recent years than in many of the neighbouring colleges. That should cause the authorities to "fear that some indignation has gone out against you which doth produce such fearful effects". The Warden and Fellows ought seriously to consider whether by prayer they should not "in humiliation expiate those sins either open or secret which may be thought to provoke the wrath of the Almighty upon you".[1]

Abbot set his face against college "resignations", which was a system of resigning with the sole object of making room for someone nominated by a patron. In 1628 he insisted on imposing on all electors an oath to make the elections freely, without any reward or gift, but this was never enforced. He himself refused to press the college to elect his nominees.

> I have been much pressed to write to your Society and to recommend towardly young men to those rooms, but ... given way to no importunity ... For I well know that you must make your elections upon oath ... and you are or should be better acquainted with those persons who stand for those places, whereas I may recommend to you those who are not so worthy or may less agree with the ordinances of your founders.[2]

One of the last acts of his life is further evidence that Abbot was not indifferent to reverence and order in public worship. In the parish of Crayford, Kent, there was controversy over the administration of Holy Communion and Abbot ordered the parishioners who intended to receive the Sacrament to do so kneeling on the steps ascending to the altar. If there was a large number of communicants, the first group, having received the Sacrament in this manner, were to return to their seats and "to give way for a second company to receive in like manner, to return and give way for a third company, and the third to the fourth, and so

---

[1] Ibid., p. 126; C. T. Martin, *Catalogue of the Archives in All Souls* (1877), p. 326.

[2] M. Burrows, *Worthies of All Souls*, pp. 132 f.

successively, until all the communicants there have received the Holy Communion in manner and time aforesaid".[1] G. W. O. Addleshaw and F. Etchells have commented on the interest of this order. It was the practice of Laudian clergy to insist on communicants kneeling at the rails instead of waiting in their seats for the clergy to come round to them, and "in spite of his Puritanism, Archbishop Abbot is ordering the Laudian method of giving Communion to be adopted".[2]

This order was dated 3 July. On the twenty-sixth Abbot became seriously ill and this time he did not recover. "The Archbishop of Canterbury is very sick and weak at Croydon, inasmuch as it is thought he will hardly escape or live long." So wrote Edward Nicholas to Captain John Pennington on 7 August,[3] but before the letter was sent he had to add as a postscript: "The Archbishop of Canterbury died on Sunday last." After long years of waiting and chafing Laud's hour had come. "On Sunday last old George of Canterbury stepped aside and lay down to sleep and up started the Bishop of good London, and put on his clothes before we were sure he was fast asleep and key cold."[4] Laud wrote in his diary: "August 4th.1633.Sunday, News came to the Court of the Lord Archbishop of Canterbury's death, and the King resolved presently to give it me."[5] Two days later Charles greeted him with the words: "My Lord's Grace of Canterbury, you are very welcome."

The funeral of the late Archbishop took place at Croydon on Tuesday 3 September when the sermon was preached by John Bowle, Bishop of Rochester.[6] He was buried, as he had desired, in the Lady Chapel of Holy Trinity Church, Guildford, and a few years later a large and elaborate tomb was erected by his brother, Sir Maurice Abbot. It incorporated an effigy of the Archbishop

[1] E. Cardwell, *Documentary Annals of the Reformed Church of England* (1839), II, pp. 175 f.

[2] G. W. O. Addleshaw and F. Etchells, *The Architectural Setting of Anglican Worship* (1948), p. 122.

[3] *S.P. Dom. Chas. I*, ccxlv, 37.

[4] W. M[ulsho] to Lord Montague, August 1633—Buccleuch MSS. (*Hist. MSS. Reports*, Series 45, I, p. 274).

[5] In *Works*, III, p. 218.

[6] Richard Kilvert to (?) Sir John Lambe, 29 Aug. 1633—*S.P. Dom. Chas. I*, ccxlv, 36.

in rochet, chimere, and cap, holding a book in his right hand, while above the effigy rose six classic columns supporting a large canopy.

When he died Abbot left all his affairs in order. Under his Will[1] he bequeathed legacies to his servants and to the poor at Lambeth and Croydon. He arranged for the sum of £20 to be paid annually to the widow of Peter Hawkins, the keeper whom he shot in 1621, for so long as she lived. Other bequests went to his relatives—to his brother John at Guildford, to his nephew Maurice, and to his niece and her husband, Sir Nathaniel and Lady Brent. Three of the Archbishop's legacies are of particular interest. The first is the sum of £100 which he left to the Princess Elizabeth (daughter of James I and wife of the Elector of the Palatinate) "to make a pretty cup of gold, in token of my dutiful respect and service to her princely dignity". This is some indication of how much his heart had been set upon her marriage to Frederick and of the sincerity of his concern that England should come to their aid in their time of trouble. The second legacy is concerned with the town of Guildford. Besides arranging for the endowment of his hospital he provided £100 to be lent to poor tradesmen of the town for two or three years. As early as 1614 he had been concerned to learn that trade was not flourishing in Guildford and, "out of my love to the place of my birth", he had written to the Mayor to ask what he could do to help. He had suggested various schemes, invited the Mayor's opinions, and arranged for £100 to be sent to him. This money was not to be spent "but to be laid up in safe custody, until such time as I shall give order for the using of the same, upon such resolution as I shall receive jointly".[2]

The third legacy of interest concerns the disposal of his library, which he left to Lambeth Palace for the use of future Archbishops. The interest lies in the light which the library throws on his interests. The majority of the books were on Church History, and the next greatest number were on Litterae Humaniores and Protestant theology and controversy. Significantly, there were

[1] Printed in *The Life of George Abbot, Lord Archbishop of Canterbury, reprinted with some Additions and Corrections from the* Biographia Britannica, *with his Character by the Right Hon. Arthur Onslow, Late Speaker of the House of Commons . . . Printed and sold by J. Russell* (1777).

[2] Abbot to the Mayor of Guildford, 13 Dec. 1614—*Life of George Abbot . . .* p. 71.

only four Puritan books. In general literature, Abbot's taste ran to writers of his own day, such as Burton, Spenser, and Montaigne, rather than to the classics. "There were also books on numismatics, architecture, and the art of warfare, but Abbot seems to have been most interested in political theory, in mathematics, in witchcraft and, above all, in France. The number of books on the history, topography, language, people and contemporary events of that country is astonishing."[1] It will be agreed that this list indicates a breadth of interests, some of them unusual and unexpected, which reveals Abbot in a new light. Lambeth also received the late Primate's pictures and maps and his barge.

It would appear that Abbot had been diligent in keeping his archiepiscopal property in good order and repair. "It appeareth to the world," he wrote in his Will,

> how careful I have been in repairing all the houses belonging to the See of Canterbury, beyond that which my predecessors have done in the memory of man, and that I have bestowed divers thousands of pounds upon the same . . . beside the care which to my great charge I have had for the preservation of the woods of the Archbishopric standing in Kent and Surrey, which I have so spared beyond my predecessors, that I have bought timber to the value of some hundreds of pounds to repair my houses, because I would not cut young trees, but let them grow up to the benefit of my successors.

[1] Ann Cox-Johnson, "Lambeth Palace Library, 1610–44", in *Transactions of the Cambridge Bibliographical Society* (1955), II, p. 108.

I I

"A Divine
of manifest Integrity"

Lord, who shall dwell in thy tabernacle: or who shall rest upon thy holy hill?
Even he that leadeth an uncorrupt life: and doeth the thing which is right, and
speaketh the truth from his heart.
He that hath used no deceit in his tongue, nor done evil to his neighbour: and
hath not slandered his neighbour. . . .
He that sweareth unto his neighbour, and disappointeth him not: though it
were to his own hindrance.
He that hath not given his money upon usury: nor taken reward against the
innocent.
Whoso doeth these things: shall never fall.

Psalm 15

GEORGE ABBOT has on the whole been unfortunately
served by those who have written of his life and character.
If Bishop Lancelot Andrewes has been unduly adulated by
his admirers, George Abbot has been unduly denigrated by his
critics. His archiepiscopate was undoubtedly a failure; faults of
character he undoubtedly had; but much of the harsh criticism
has come from admirers of William Laud who have sought to
find, in depreciating the character of Abbot, added reason for
extolling the reputation of Laud. One of the earliest estimates of
Abbot was given by Hammond L'Estrange in a work published
in 1655.[1] It was highly critical and it was copied into various
subsequent works. Peter Heylyn and David Lloyd both used it
and through them it became the "accepted" portrait of the
Archbishop. At the same time there have not been wanting other
writers who presented a completely different picture of the
Archbishop's character, but their assessment has failed to carry
much weight against Abbot's detractors.[2]

[1] *The Reign of King Charles.*
[2] For a selection of estimates of Archbishop Abbot, see Appendix.

Abbot was elevated to the Primacy at a moment when there was moving through the Church of England a concern for a theology which would justify her independent existence and thus equip her to meet the militancy of both Calvinism and Romanism with an equally militant Anglicanism. To this end, men like Richard Hooker,[1] John Jewel,[2] and Lancelot Andrewes[3] sought to show that the Church of England had its own theological basis in Scripture and in the history of the first five Christian centuries. They and their followers did not believe, as many had done in the years immediately succeeding the Reformation, that England must choose between a return to Rome and a more radical acceptance of Calvinism. On the contrary, the Church of England had discarded the corruptions and errors of Rome, but—as Bishop Jewel wrote—"we have called home again to the original and first foundation, that religion which hath been foully foreslowed, and utterly corrupted by these men". In a famous passage in one of his sermons Lancelot Andrewes summarized the Anglican position thus:

> One canon reduced to writing by God himself, two testaments, three creeds, four general councils, five centuries, and the series of Fathers in that period—the centuries, that is, before Constantine, and two after, determine the boundary of our faith.[4]

In thus justifying the independent position of Anglicanism its apologists were led to attack both the novelties of Rome and the radicalism of the Puritans. The Church of England held as *de fide* neither more nor less than did the Fathers and therefore she must reject the Popish novelties which had added to the Faith and the Puritan radicalism which would tolerate nothing apart from the Scriptures.

Most of those who held this theological position, and who were sometimes known as Arminians, also possessed a high theological conception of the nature of Kingship. They saw in the Old

---

[1] *Laws of Ecclesiastical Polity,* 1594–1662, in *Works* (ed. J. Keble, 1836).

[2] *Apology of the Church of England,* 1562, in *Works* (ed. J. Ayre, 1848).

[3] *Tortura Torti* (1609); *Responsio ad Apologiam Cardinalis Bellarmine* (1610), in *Works* (ed. J. Bliss, 1851).

[4] In 1613—*Opuscula Quaedam Posthuma* (1852), p. 91.

Testament idea of the "godly prince" a bulwark against the political and ecclesiastical pretensions of both the Papacy and the Presbytery. G. Kitson Clark has noted that

> both Papist and Presbyterian were at least agreed in this. They believed that Christ had instituted a Church which was endowed with a right to command the secular authority, even where he is a king, to impose its own religious pattern on society, and, if necessary, to use for that purpose the sword of persecution.[1]

It is not surprising, therefore, that because of their lofty conception of Kingship, the defenders of an independent Anglicanism found support from the monarch. Both James I and Charles I themselves held the same exalted view of their own office. Consequently the Arminians began to be summoned to positions of influence in Church and State. The process increased rapidly after Charles became King, with Laud as his chief adviser in ecclesiastical affairs. It increased to such an extent that it became a prime source of complaint by the Commons in the Parliamentary session in 1629.[2] For it was an ominous fact that the majority of people saw in the rising tide of Arminianism a great threat to the Reformation settlement. To them it represented a deviation from pure Reformed doctrine and the thin end of the wedge of Romanism. They also strongly disliked the growing political power of individual bishops. All this concentrated opposition against the Caroline episcopate.

George Abbot was one of this majority. He never wavered from his Calvinistic theological position, although he was unlike many of his fellow-Calvinists in his acceptance of episcopacy and of the need for a modicum of uniformity in worship. Like the rest of the Puritan wing he saw in the growing power of Arminianism a threat to Calvinism, and to him the immediate need was for resolution to defend the Church of England against "her

[1] G. Kitson Clark, *The English Inheritance* (1950), p. 53.
[2] Manwaring, who had been forbidden by Parliament to hold any ecclesiastical preferment again, now held the rectory of St Giles-in-the-Fields, Richard Montague had been appointed Bishop of Chichester, Neile had been brought nearer to the centre of influence by his translation from Durham to Winchester, Mountain had been banished to Durham to make room for Laud at London, and White, who had licensed Montague's controversial book, had been elevated from Carlisle to Norwich.

false brethren, like Arminians, who would betray her".[1] With what result? His sternness towards Arminians and Papists at home and his defence and support of Protestants abroad ran counter to much of James's foreign policy, which involved courting the Catholic powers, and to his home policy, which, linked as it was with his foreign policy, involved tactful dealings with Papists. Thus Abbot could not depend for influence and support upon James, who turned for advice elsewhere. Still less could he rely upon Charles I, and soon his most influential colleagues on the bench were antagonistic to him and he to them. Thus we have the spectacle of the impotent Archbishop. Neither James (after the Essex Divorce) nor Charles wanted an archbishop of Abbot's mould, while the effective policy-makers of the Church found him an impediment and an encumbrance. So the Church of England was for twenty-two years deprived of effective leadership. Had Laud become Archbishop earlier than 1633 it is possible that the absence of years of frustration might have enabled him to put his policy into operation with less fury and harshness than he did in 1633. On the other hand, the crisis which developed after 1633 might have been precipitated. What the Church needed in 1611 was an archbishop whose sympathies were less Calvinistic than Abbot's—one who, while he would be acceptable to the monarch and sympathetic to the Arminians, would yet be sufficiently a statesman to lead rather than to drive the Church to a more independent understanding of itself—one who would follow Bancroft in welding the parties in the Church into some semblance of unity. It is even possible to envisage one of Abbot's theological persuasion, who was also an able administrator, a strong character, and a statesman, leading the Church away from Arminianism and thus avoiding the excesses which afterwards proved so injurious to it. But that is entirely a hypothetical situation, for no man could have suppressed Arminianism so long as the King was who he was and what he was. We must, therefore, accept the conclusion of Hugh Trevor-Roper that the result of Abbot's archiepiscopate

> was that the problem of an ecclesiastical policy, which was now
> realised to be pressing, was deferred for more than ten years,

[1] John Rogan, "King James's Bishops", in *Durham University Journal* (June 1956), p. 94.

while Abbot's rule was not strong enough to prevent the two parties from becoming more antagonistic by opposition.[1]

As for Abbot himself, he held that "this famous Church of England" was "the best framed pattern of all the churches of Europe".[2] It is unfortunate that he did so little to keep it so.

It was not Abbot's theological position alone which weakened his influence. He was a far better man than he was an archbishop, but here too certain traits led to unpopularity at the centre of influence. His very virtues proved to be his public undoing. He was a man possessed of a conscience which would not bow to the royal will. Unlike Andrewes, he was utterly consistent throughout his career. Unlike Andrewes again, he had the moral courage to defy the King's command if conscience required it. He never wavered in his opposition to the Essex Divorce. That opposition was based on moral scruples and in adhering to it he largely lost the goodwill of James I. He never wavered in his refusal to license Sibthorpe's sermon. That opposition was based on moral scruples and in adhering to it he increased the ill will of Charles I. This constancy of moral purpose and resistance to unjust authority was thus another factor which led to his waning influence. In the words of G. M. Trevelyan, "Archbishop Abbot, after long trying, like William Penn in later days, to combine influence at a bad Court, with the conscience of a good man, fell into honourable disgrace."[3]

It would appear that Abbot's personality was not the most attractive. Clarendon described him as a man of "very morose manners and a very sour aspect which, in that time, was called gravity".[4] Allowing for Clarendon's lack of sympathy for Abbot, there is probably some degree of truth in his description. His sincere sense of moral uprightness, which conveyed to many an impression of stubbornness, and his strict Calvinism made him gloomy and narrow-minded, and this in turn "made his views more unpalatable without enabling him to win friends".[5]

[1] H. Trevor-Roper, *Archbishop Laud* (1940), p. 42.
[2] In his Will.
[3] *England under the Stuarts* (1904), p. 110.
[4] *History of the Great Rebellion* (1717), I, p. 88.
[5] John Rogan, "King James's Bishops", in *Durham University Journal* (June 1956), p. 94.

Abbot has been charged with laxity in enforcing conformity.

His extraordinary remissness in not exacting strict conformity to the prescribed orders of the Church in point of ceremony, seemed to resolve those legal determinations to their first principle of indifferency, and led in such a habit of inconformity, as the future reduction of those tender conscience'd men to long discontinued obedience, was interpreted an innovation.[1]

Now there is little evidence for such a sweeping judgement, and certain facts point in the other direction. His *Visitation Articles*[2] reveal that he was as much concerned as his fellow-bishops to seek out cases where there was lack of order in the worship of the Church, where conventicles were held, and where unauthorized persons had been permitted to minister. In 1633 on the High Commission he had showed his dislike of the right claimed by the parishioners of St Austin's, London, to seats above the Communion table,[3] and almost the last act of his life was to issue an order for observing decency at the reception of Holy Communion at Crayford.[4] Calvinist though he was, he had no love for the factiousness of the extreme Puritans, and the part he played in preparing the way for the extension of episcopacy in Scotland shows that he had no sympathy with their conceptions of Church Order. But if it is untrue to assert that he was lax in his enforcement of conformity, there is no doubt that he was moderate in his dealings with Puritans. "In all his conduct [he] showed an unwillingness to stretch the act of *uniformity* beyond what was absolutely necessary for the peace of the *Church*, or the *prerogative* of the crown, any further than conduced to the good will of the *state*."[5]

It is not here that we must look for Abbot's weakness. That lay rather in his apparent lack of concern as to where the Church was going. He was no administrator, he was no reformer, he had no gift for consolidation. We see him in the context of the State, where he did not shine, rather than in the context of the Church,

---

[1] Hammond L'Estrange, *The Reign of King Charles* (1655), p. 131, accepted by P. Heylyn, *Cyprianus Anglicus,* p. 242.

[2] See above, pp. 41 ff.   [3] See above, p. 140.   [4] See above, pp. 143 f.

[5] J. Welwood, *Memoirs of the most material transactions in England, for the last 100 years* (1700), p. 38.

where he was impotent. It was this bias towards affairs of State which lay behind Thomas Fuller's criticism that "in his house he respected his secretary above his chaplains, and out of it always honoured cloaks above cassocks, lay above clergymen".[1] It is possible that his lack of parochial experience was responsible for this bias. Peter Heylyn has a well-known sentence that Abbot

> having never been Parson, Vicar, nor Curate, he was altogether ignorant of those afflications which the Clergy do too often suffer by the pride of some, and the Avarice of others of their Country Neighbours, and consequently showed the least compassion towards them when any of them had the hard fortune to be brought before him.[2]

Certainly this inexperience led to severity. The reason which he himself was said to have offered for his sternness was somewhat uncomplimentary to the clergy themselves. "This he endeavoured to excuse to a private friend, by protesting himself so severe to the Clergy on purpose to rescue them from the severity of others, and to prevent them from Lay Judges to their greater shame."[3] Abbot was by no means the only bishop to reach eminence without parochial experience, but, in spite of the fact that in his early days he had a penetrating insight into the problems of the parochial clergy,[4] in his later years he seems to have become deficient in the one quality which can make up for lack of experience—the gift of imagination. "His mind was deficient in breadth and geniality, and he never could have acquired the capacity for entering into the arguments and feeling of an opponent, which is the first requisite for public life."[5]

Such were the defects of character and the accidents of circumstances which contributed to the impotency of Abbot's archiepiscopate. Fundamentally, however, he was a good and conscientious man. He had neither the insincerity of Williams, the harshness of Laud, nor the weakness of Andrewes. He was kindly and hospitable, his piety was deep and genuine, he was

---

[1] *Worthies of England* (ed. J. Freeman, 1952), p. 552.
[2] *Cyprianus Anglicus,* pp. 243 f.
[3] T. Fuller, *Church History of Britain* (1655), Bk. xi, sec. i, par. 54.
[4] See above, p. 13.
[5] S. R. Gardiner, *History of England, 1603–42* (1883–4), II, p. 121.

void of unnecessary pomp and ostentation. He was an excellent preacher and a careful steward of the properties of his See. He was not avaricious and had none of the zeal for amassing prefer-ments which was displayed by Vaughan, Harsnet, Neile, or Williams. On the contrary, he was generous to the poor and to those communities and institutions with which he had to do. Above all there shines out his scrupulous conscientiousness and his moral courage. He was "a divine of manifest integrity, with that consciousness of right which was found so often in his school of thought".[1]

[1] D. Mathew, *The Jacobean Age* (1938), p. 95.

Appendix

A SELECTION OF ESTIMATES OF THE CHARACTER OF ABBOT

HAMMOND L'ESTRANGE, 1655

"A very learned man he was, his erudition all of the old stamp, stiffly principled in the doctrine of *St Augustine* in which they who understand it not, call *Calvinism*. . . . Pious, grave, and exemplary in his conversation. But some think a better Man than Archbishop, and that he was better qualified with merit for the dignity, than with a spirit answering the function, in the exercise whereof he was conceived too facile and yielding; his extraordinary remissness in not exacting strict conformity to the prescribed orders of the Church in point of ceremony, seemed to resolve those legal determinations to their first principle of indifferency, and led in such a habit of inconformity, as the future reduction of those tender conscience'd men to long discontinued obedience, was interpreted an innovation. This was the height of what I dare report his failings reached to."

The Reign of King Charles, p. 127

THOMAS FULLER, 1662

"I find two things much charged on his memory: first that in his house he respected his secretary above his chaplains, and out of it always honoured cloaks above cassocks, lay above clergymen; secondly that he connived at the spreading of non-conformity, insomuch that I read in a modern author, 'Had Bishop Laud succeeded Bancroft, and the project of conformity been followed without interruption, there is little question to be made but that our Jerusalem (by this time) might have been a city at unity in itself.'

"Yet are there some of Abbot's relatives, who (as I am

155

informed) will undertake to defend him, that he was in no way guilty of these crimes laid to his charge."

The Worthies of England, p. 552 (1952 ed.)

DAVID LLOYD, 1665

"To say the truth, he was a man of good intentions, and knew much, but failed in what those ordinarily do that are devoted to our modern singularities, being extremely obstinate in his opinions, which the King was more willing to understand than follow, because most time he looked upon things according to the rigour of ecclesiastic maxims, and was either too curious and irresolute by variety of reading, or too peremptory and positive from the strictness of his rules; or too zealous by reason of the seriousness of his study; or wide from the matter by reason of his inexperience, and aptness to require in the times he lived, the regularity of the times he read of, heeding not the force of circumstances, the errors of comparison, or the caution of application. . . . His principles betrayed his profession, which he rendered too obnoxious, while he supported it by those novel grounds which our adversaries could make us confess were heterodox, and by those straight-laced foundations which we saw ourselves too narrow. . . . Some think him a better man than archbishop. . . . "

State Worthies from the Reformation to the Restoration (1766 ed.), II, pp. 34 f

JAMES WELWOOD, 1700

"He was a person of wonderful temper and moderation; and in all his conduct, showed an unwillingness to stretch the act of *uniformity* beyond what was absolutely necessary for the peace of the *Church,* or the *prerogative* of the Crown, any farther than conduced to the good of the *state.* Being not well turned for a court, though otherwise of considerable learning and genteel education, he either could not, or would not, stoop to the humour of the times; and now and then, by an unseasonable stiffness, gave occasion to his enemies to represent him, as not well inclined to the *prerogative,* or too much addicted to a *popular interest*: and therefore not fit to be employed in matters of government."

Memoirs of the most material transactions in England for the last 100 years, p. 38

APPENDIX

THE EARL OF CLARENDON, 1702

"The remissness of *Abbot* and of other Bishops by his example, had introduced, or at least conniv'd at a Negligence, that gave great scandal to the Church, and no doubt offended many Pious men. . . . He was a Man of very Morose manners and a very sour aspect, which, at that time, was called Gravity. . . . For the strict observation of the Discipline of the Church, or the Conformity to the Articles, or Canons established, he made little inquiry, and took less care. . . . That temper in the Archbishop, whose House was a Sanctuary to the most eminent of that Factious Party, and who Licenced their most Pernicious Writings, left his Successor a very difficult work to do, to Reform, and Reduce a Church into Order, that had been so long neglected."

History of the Great Rebellion (1717 ed.), II, pp. 95, 88 f

THE RIGHT HON. ARTHUR ONSLOW, 1723

"He was a wise and prudent man, knew well the temper and disposition of the kingdom with respect to the ceremonies and power of the church, and did, therefore, use a moderation in the point of ecclesiastical discipline, which if it had been followed by his successor, the ruin that soon after fell on the church, might very likely have been prevented. . . . He was eminent for piety and care for the poor, and his hospitality fully answered the injunction King James laid upon him, which was to live like an Archbishop and to carry his house nobly. He had no thoughts of heaping up riches. . . . He was void of all pomp and ostentation; and thought the nearer the church and churchmen came to the simplicity of the first Christians the better would the true ends of religion be served, and that the purity of the heart was to be preferred to, and ought rather to be the care of a spiritual governor than the devotion of the hands only. If under this notion some niceties in discipline were given up to goodness of life, and when the peace of the Church as well as of the kingdom was preserved by it, 'twas surely no ill piece of prudence, nor is his memory therefore deserving of those slanders it has undergone on that account. . . .

"[Abbot and Laud] were indeed men of different frames, and the parts they took in the affairs both of Church and State as

157

disagreeing. In the Church moderation and the ways of grace guided the behaviour of the first, rigour and severity that of the last. . . .

"The one made the liberty of the people and laws of the land the measure of his actions, when the other, to speak softly of it, had the power of the Prince and the exalting prerogative only, for the foundation of his. They were indeed both of them men of courage and resolution; but it was sedate and temperate in Abbot, passionate and unruly in Laud."

The Character of Archbishop Abbot, upon reading Lord Clarendon's Account of him

S. R. Gardiner, 1883

"His piety was deep and real, and his thorough conscientiousness was such that it might safely be predicted that, whatever mistakes he might make in his new office, neither fear nor interest would induce him to swerve for a moment from what he considered to be the strict line of duty.

"These merits were balanced by faults. . . . It was observed of him that he had never had personal experience of pastoral duties. . . . His mind was deficient in breadth and geniality, and he never could have acquired the capacity for entering into the arguments and feeling of an opponent, which is the first requisite in public life. His theology was the theology of the Puritans. . . . In his hands, if he had been allowed to have his will, the Church of England would have become as one-sided as it afterwards became in the hands of his opponents."

History of England, 1603-42, II, pp. 121 f

Bibliography

PART I

WORKS BY ABBOT:

Questiones sex totidem praelectionibus in Schola Theologica Oxoniae, pro forma habitis, discussae et disceptatae anno 1597, in quibus e Sacra Scriptura et Patribus, quid statuendum sit definitur. 1598.

An Exposition on the Prophet Jonah, in certain Sermons preached at St Mary's Church in Oxford. 1600.

The Reasons which Doctor Hill hath brought for the upholding of Papistry, which is falsely termed the Catholic Religion, unmasked, and showed to be very weak, and upon examination most insufficient for that purpose. 1604.

A Brief Description of the Whole World. 1605.

A Sermon Preached at Westminster, May 26, 1608, at the Funeral Solemnities of the Right Hon. Thomas Earl of Dorset. 1608.

The Examination, Arraignment and Conviction of George Sprot . . . written and set forth by Sir William Hart . . . Before which Treatise is also prefixed a Preface, written by G. Abbot, Doctor of Divinity, and Dean of Winchester, who was present at the said Sprot's execution. 1608.

Articles to be inquired of, in the first Metropolitical Visitation of the most Revd Father, George . . . Archbishop of Canterbury . . . in, and for, the diocese of Lincoln, in the year of our Lord, 1613. 1613.

A Treatise of the Perpetual Visibility and the Succession of the True Church in All Ages. 1624.

Account, written by Dr George Abbot, Archbishop of Canterbury, with the Speech he intended to have made, and King James's Letter to him [Essex Divorce]. 1613. Printed in W. Cobbett, *Complete Collection of State Trials* (1809), Vol. II, pp. 806 ff.

Cheapside Cross Censured and Condemned by a Letter sent from the Vice-Chancellor and other Learned Men of the famous University of Oxford in Answer to a Question propounded by the Citizens of London, concerning the said Cross, in the year 1600, in which year it was beautified . . . 1641.

Archbishop Abbot his Narrative [concerning his Sequestration]. 1627. Printed in J. Rushworth, *Historical Collections . . .* (1721), Vol. I, pp. 434 ff, and in W. Cobbett, *Complete Collection of State Trials,* Vol. II, pp. 1451 ff.

WORKS AND ARTICLES ON ABBOT:

ABBOT, John Thomas. *An Apology for Dr. George Abbot, Lord Archbishop of Canterbury, As touching some Strictures on his Memory.* 1863.

Anonymous Article in *The Churchman's Family Magazine,* February 1863.

AUBREY, John. In *Brief Lives* (ed. O. L. Dick, 1949). Originally written 1669.

CUNNINGHAM, G. D. In *Lives of Eminent and Illustrious Englishmen,* Vol. VIII, 1838.

FOX, A. W. In *A Book of Bachelors.* 1899.

FULLER, Thomas. In *The Worthies of England* (ed. J. Freeman, 1952). First published in 1662.

HOOK, W. F. "George Abbot", in *An Ecclesiastical Biography* (1845–52), Vol. I.

—— In *Lives of the Archbishops of Canterbury,* Vol. X, 1875.

Life of George Abbot . . . reprinted with some Additions and Corrections from the Biographia Britannica, *with his Character by the Right Hon. Arthur Onslow, Late Speaker of the House of Commons . . . Printed and sold by John Russell.* 1777.

LEE, S. L. "George Abbot", in *Dictionary of National Biography.*

LLOYD, David. In *State Worthies from the Reformation to the Revolution.* 1766.

OLDYS, William. "George Abbot", in *Biographia Britannica,* Vol. I, 1788.

ONSLOW, Arthur. *The Character of Archbishop Abbot upon reading Lord Clarendon's Account of him.* 1723.

A Short Apology for Archbishop Abbot, touching the death of Peter Hawkins. By an Unknown hand. 1621. Printed in *The English Works of Sir Henry Spelman* (ed. Edmund Gibson, 1727).

SPELMAN, Sir Henry. *An Answer to the Foregoing Apology* [touching the death of Peter Hawkins]. 1621. Printed in *The English Works of Sir Henry Spelman* (ed. Edmund Gibson, 1727).

Some Observable Things, since September 25, 1613, when the Sentence was given in the cause of the Earl of Essex, continued unto the day of the Marriage, December 26, 1613. 1613. Printed in W. Cobbett, *Complete Collection of State Trials,* Vol. II, pp. 829 ff.

WEBSTER, Grace. "Life of George Abbot", in Abbot's *Exposition on the Prophet Jonah* (ed. J. Webster, 1845), Vol. I.

WRANGHAM, Francis. In *The British Plutarch,* Vol. II, 1816.

NOTE

For a full bibliographical study of works by and on Abbot, see:

CHRISTOPHERS, R. A. *A Bibliography of George Abbot, Archbishop of Canterbury.* Unpublished thesis for the University of London Diploma in Librarianship. May 1960.

BIBLIOGRAPHY

PART II

MANUSCRIPT SOURCES

BODLEIAN LIBRARY, OXFORD
Rawlinson MSS.
Tanner MSS.

BALLIOL COLLEGE, OXFORD
College Registers.

BRITISH MUSEUM, LONDON
Baker MSS.
Harleian MSS.
Sloane MSS.
Additional MSS.

GUILDHALL LIBRARY, LONDON
Registers of the Bishops of London.
MSS. 9531/15, f. 392.

LAMBETH PALACE, LONDON
Archbishop Abbot's Registers.
MSS. 943/77, 103, 105.

UNIVERSITY COLLEGE, OXFORD
College Registers.

PRINTED WORKS

COLLECTIONS OF OFFICIAL DOCUMENTS, CALENDARS, REGISTERS, ACTS, ETC.

Acts of the Privy Council of England.
Acts of the Privy Council of Scotland.
Balliol College Annual Lists, compiled by Andrew Clark. 1909.
Calendar of State Papers, Domestic: Elizabeth I, James I, Charles I.
Calendar of State Papers, Foreign: Venice.
CARDWELL, E. *Documentary Annals of the Reformed Church of England.*
    1839.
COBBETT, W. *Complete Collection of State Trials,* Vol. II. 1809.
GARDINER, S. R. (ed.) *Notes on the Debates in the House of Lords, 1621.*
    1870.

BIBLIOGRAPHY

GARDINER, S. R. *Notes on the Debates in the House of Lords, 1624 and 1626.* 1879.
—— *Reports of Cases in the Courts of Star Chamber and High Commission.* 1886.
Lords, Journals of the House of, Vols. II and III.
MARTIN, C. T. *Catalogue of the Archives in All Souls.* 1877.
RELF, F. H. (ed.) *Notes on the Debates in the House of Lords 1621, 1625, 1628.* 1929.
Royal Commission on Historical Manuscripts:
  Reports: Series 23. Cowper MSS. 1888–9.
           45. Buccleuch MSS. 1889–1926.
           75. Downshire MSS. 1924–42.
TANNER, J. R. *Constitutional Documents of the Reign of James I.* 1930.
WILKINS, D. *Concilia Magnae Britanniae et Hiberniae, 444–1718,* Vol. IV. 1737.

CONTEMPORARY WORKS

Letters, Papers, and Diaries

ATTERBURY, L. (ed.) *Some Letters relating to the History of the Council of Trent.* 1705.
BIRCH, T. *The Court and Times of James I.* 1848.
—— *The Court and Times of Charles I.* 1849.
BODLEY, Sir Thomas. *Letters.* Ed. C. W. Wheeler, 1927.
—— *Letters to Thomas James, 1st Keeper of the Bodleian Library.* Ed. C. W. Wheeler, 1926.
Cabala. Mysteries of State, in Letters of the great Ministers of King James and King Charles. 1654.
CHAMBERLAIN, John. *Letters during the reign of Queen Elizabeth.* Ed. S. Williams, 1861.
—— *Letters.* Ed. N. E. McClure, 1939.
CROSFIELD, Thomas. *Diary.* Ed. F. S. Boas, 1935.
Egerton Papers, The. Ed. J. P. Collier, 1840.
EPISCOPUS, Simon. *Praestantium ac eruditorum virorum epistolae ecclesiasticae . . .* 1660.
Fortescue Papers, The. Ed. S. R. Gardiner. 1871.
GERARD, John. *The Autobiography of an Elizabethan.* Trans. Philip Caraman. 1951.
LAING, D. (ed.) *Original Letters relating to Ecclesiastical Affairs in Scotland.* 1851.
MANNINGHAM, John. *Diary.* Ed. J. Bruce, 1868.
Sidney Papers, The. [Letters and Memorials of state . . . from the originals at Penshurst, etc.] Ed. A. Collins, 1746.

WILLIAMS, John. *Letters of Archbishop Williams, and others addressed to him.* 1864.
YONGE, Walter. *Diary.* Ed. G. Roberts, 1848.

Tracts, Pamphlets, Sermons, etc.
BRISTOW, Richard. *A Brief Treatise of divers plain and sure ways to find out the truth in this doubtful and dangerous time of Heresy. Containing sundry worthy motives unto the Catholic Faith.* 1599.
CLARE, John. *The Converted Jew or certain dialogues between Michaeas a Learned Jew, and others, touching divers points of Religion, controverted between Catholics and Protestants.* 1630. Appendix.
DILLINGHAM, Francis. *A Quartron of Reasons, composed by Doctor Hill, unquartered, and proved a quartron of follies.* 1603.
HILL, T. *A Quartron of reasons of Catholic Religion.* 1600.
MANWARING, Roger. *Religion and Allegiance: in two Sermons, preached before the King's Majesty* . . . 1627.
MONTAGUE, Richard. *A New Gag for an Old Goose.* 1624.
—— *Appello Caesarem.* 1625.
OVERALL, John. *Bishop Overall's Convocation Book.* Published in 1689 under the title *Concerning the Government of God's Catholic Church and the Kingdoms of the whole world.*
PAGE, William. *A Treatise or justification of bowing at the name of Jesus.* 1631.
PRYNNE, William. *Lame Giles, His Haltings.* 1631.
SCOTT, W. (ed.). *Collection of Scarce and Valuable Tracts (Somers Tracts).* 1809–15.
SIBTHORPE, Robert. *Apostolic Obedience. Showing the Duty of Subjects to pay Tribute and Taxes to their Princes, according to the Word of God, in the Law and the Gospel and the Rules of Religion* . . . .*A Sermon preached at Northampton.* . . . *Feb. 22nd,* 1627.
Survey of the Book of Common Prayer, by an anonymous author. 2nd. ed. 1610.
WIDDOWES, Giles. *The Lawless Kneelingless Schismatical Puritan.* 1630.

Collected Works
LAUD, William. *Works.* Ed. W. Scott and J. Bliss, 1847–60.
BACON, Francis. *Works.* Ed. J. Spedding and others, 1857–74.
SPELMAN, Henry. *English Works.* Ed. Edmund Gibson, 1727.

Collections of contemporary historical documents
Abbotsford Club, Miscellany of the. 1837.
COLLINS, A. (ed). *Letters and Memorials of State in the Reigns of Queen Mary, Queen Elizabeth, James I.,* etc., Vol. II. 1746.

NICHOLS, John (ed.). *The Progresses, Processions, and Magnificent Festivities of King James the First* . . . 1828.

RUSHWORTH, John. *Historical Collections of private passages of state, weighty matters in law, remarkable precedents in five parliaments* . . . 1721.

WINWOOD, R. *Memorials of affairs of State in the reign of Queen Elizabeth and King James I.* Ed. J. Sawyer, 1725.

WORDSWORTH, C. (ed.). *Manner of the Coronation of King Charles I.* 1892.

LATER WORKS

ADDLESHAW, G. W. O. *The High Church Tradition.* 1941.

—— and ETCHELLS, F. *The Architectural Setting of Anglican Worship.* 1948.

ALLEN, J. W. *English Political Thought, 1603–1660,* Vol. I. 1938.

Archaeologia Cantiana, Vol. 42. 1930.

AUBREY, J. *Brief Lives.* Ed. O. L. Dick, 1949. Originally written 1669, first published 1813.

BAILEY, J. E. *The Life of Thomas Fuller.* 1874.

BOWEN, C. D. *The Lion and the Throne.* 1957.

BURRAGE, C. *The English Dissenters in the Light of Recent Research.* 1912.

BURROWS, M. *Worthies of All Souls.* 1874.

CARR, J. A. *Life and Times of James Ussher.* 1895.

CARR, William. *University College, Oxford.* 1902.

CLARENDON, Earl of. *History of the Great Rebellion.* 1717 ed. First published 1702.

COX-JOHNSON, Ann. "Lambeth Palace Library, 1610–44", in *Transactions of the Cambridge Bibliographical Society,* Vol. II, 1955.

CURTIS, M. H. *Oxford and Cambridge in Transition, 1558-1662.* 1959.

DAICHES, D. *The King James Version of the English Bible.* 1941.

DAVIS, H. W. C. *Balliol College, Oxford.* 1899.

Dictionary of National Biography.

DONALDSON, Gordon. *The Scottish Reformation.* 1960.

ELRINGTON, C. R. *The Life of James Ussher.* 1848.

FOSTER, J. *Alumni Oxonienses.* 1887–9.

FRENCH, Allen. *Charles I and the Puritan Upheaval.* 1955.

FRERE, W. H. *The English Church in the Reigns of Elizabeth and James I.* 1924.

FULLER, Thomas. *Abel Redivivus.* 1651.

—— *Church History of Britain.* 1655.

—— *The Worthies of England.* Ed. J. Freeman, 1952. First published 1662.

GARDINER, S. R. *History of England, 1603–42,* Vols. II–IV, 1883–4.
GOODMAN, G. *The Court of King James I.* Ed. J. S. Brewer, 1839.
GOSSE, E. W. *Life and Letters of John Donne.* 1899.
HACKET, J. *Scrinia Reserata. A Memorial offered to the great deservings of John Williams.* 1692.
HANNAN, T. "The Scottish Consecrations in London in 1610", in *Church Quarterly Review.* January 1911.
HARRISON, A. W. *The Beginnings of Arminianism.* 1926.
—— *Arminianism.* 1937.
HEYLYN, Peter. *Cyprianus Anglicus.* 1668.
HILL, Christopher. *Economic Problems of the Church.* 1956.
HUTTON, W. H. *The English Church from the Accession of Charles I to the Death of Queen Anne.* 1903.
JORDAN, W. K. *The Development of Religious Toleration in England, 1603–1640.* 1932.
KINGSBURY, S. M. (ed.). *Records of the Virginia Company of London.* 1906.
NEVE, John Le. *Fasti Ecclesiae Anglicanae.* 1854.
L'ESTRANGE, Hammond. *The Reign of King Charles.* 1655.
LLOYD, David. *State Worthies from the Reformation to the Revolution.* 1766. First published 1665.
McELWEE, W. *The Murder of Sir Thomas Overbury.* 1952.
McCLEANE, D. *Pembroke College, Oxford.* 1897.
—— *Pembroke College, Oxford.* 1900.
MALLET, C. E. *History of the University of Oxford.* Vols. I and II, 1924.
MATHEW, David. *The Jacobean Age.* 1938.
—— *The Age of Charles I.* 1951.
MOIR, T. L. *The Addled Parliament of 1614.* 1958.
PARR, Richard. *Life of James Ussher.* 1687.
PATTISON, M. *Isaac Casaubon.* 1892.
ROBERTSON, C. Grant. *All Souls' College, Oxford.* 1899.
ROGAN, John. "King James's Bishops", in *Durham University Journal.* June 1956.
ROGGE, H. *Jan Wtenbogaert.* Vol. II, 1874–6.
SAVAGE, HENRY. *Balliofergus, or a Commentary upon the Foundation, Founders and Affairs of Balliol College.* 1668.
SODEN, Geoffrey. *Godfrey Goodman, Bishop of Gloucester, 1583–1656.* 1953.
SPOTTISWOODE, J. *The History of the Church of Scotland.* 1655.
TAYLOR, E. G. R. *Late Tudor and Early Stuart Geography.* 1934.
TREVELYAN, G. M. *England under the Stuarts.* 1904.
TREVOR-ROPER, Hugh. *Archbishop Laud.* 1940.
—— "King James and his Bishops", in *History Today.* September 1955.

BIBLIOGRAPHY

TURNER, E. R. *The Privy Council of England in the 17th and 18th Centuries.* Vol. I, 1927.

USHER, R. G. *The Reconstruction of the English Church.* 1910.

—— *The Rise and Fall of the High Commission.* 1913.

Victoria County History. Surrey. Vol. III, 1905.

WALE, E. G. R. *The Hospital of the Blessed Trinity, Guildford.* 1933.

WEDGWOOD, C. V. *The Thirty Years War.* 1938.

WELWOOD, James. *Memoirs of the most material transactions in England for the last 100 years.* 1700.

WELSBY, Paul A. *Lancelot Andrewes, 1555–1626.* 1958.

WILLSON, D. H. *King James VI and I.* 1956.

WOOD, Anthony à. *Athenae Oxonienses.* Vol. II, 1815.

Index

Index

Abbot, Alice (*née* March or Marsh), 3
Abbot, George: birth, 3; family, 4;
baptism, 5; attends school, 5;
scholar of Balliol College, Oxford,
5; B.A., 5; Fellow of Balliol, 5; M.A.,
5; D.D., 5; interest in geography,
7 ff; sermons on Jonah, 9 ff; preaches
in Temple Church, 14 f; preaches
at funeral of Earl of Dorset, 15;
relationship with Dorset, 17 f;
Dean of Winchester, 18; Master of
University College, Oxford, 18 f;
Vice-Chancellor, 19 f, 29; in controversy concerning crucifix at
Cheapside, 19 f; and the Essex
rebellion, 20 f; controversy with
Laud, 21 ff; meets John Gerard,
23 f; controversy with Dr Hill,
24 ff; translator of the Bible, 26;
finds patron in Earl of Dunbar,
28 f; attends James I on visit to
Oxford, 29; receives letter from
King about Overall's *Convocation
Book,* 29 f; visits Scotland, 30 f;
attends trial and execution of
Sprot, 31 f; defends King's version of Gowrie Conspiracy, 31;
Bp of Lichfield & Coventry, 32 f;
Bp of London, 33; presides at
consecration of Scottish bps, 33 f;
represses Romanism, 34, 80; takes
seat in Lords, 34; appointed Abp
of Canterbury, 36 ff; enthronement
40; relationship with diocese of
Canterbury, 40 f; with city and
Corporation, 41, 128; Visitations,
41 f; Lambeth Palace library, 42,

145; on High Commission, 43,
132, 139 f; on Privy Council, 43;
conflict with Coke, 43 ff; trial and
excution of Legate, 46 f; Arminian
controversy in Holland, 47 f;
opinion of Grotius, 49 f; relations
with Casaubon, 50; with Queen
Anne and Prince Henry, 50;
member of anti-Howard faction,
51; opposes Savoy and Spanish
marriages, 51, 80, 84, 107 ff;
present at death and funeral of
Prince Henry, 52 f; officiates at
betrothal of Princess Elizabeth,
53; entertains Elector Frederick,
53 f; officiates at marriage of
Princess Elizabeth, 54; shares in
founding London Charterhouse,
54; Visitor of All Souls College,
Oxford, 54, 83, 142 f; Chancellor
of Trinity College, Dublin, 55 f;
Essex divorce case, ch. 5 *passim*;
attends Parliament (1614), 74 ff;
causes downfall of Northampton,
76 f; introduces Villiers to King,
77; attempt on his life, 77 f; urges
Queen to commend Villiers to
King, 78 f; advises Villiers, 79 f;
takes interest in two friars converted to Church of England, 80 f;
in favour of summoning Parliament, 81 f; absolves Marquis of
Huntley, 82 f; excluded from
Spanish marriage discussions, 84;
death of his brother, Robert, 84;
opposes *Declaration of Sports,* 84 f;
case of Wraynham, 85; present at

169

Abbot, George—*cont.*
death and funeral of Queen, 86; delivers judgement against Suffolk, 86; establishes Hospital at Guildford, 87; urges intervention in Bohemia, 87 ff; raises money for relief of Frederick, 88; and the Parliament of 1621, 89; his homicide, ch. 7 *passim*; examines Abp of Spalato, 105 ff; commends King's "Directions concerning Preachers", 107; forged letter attributed to him, 108 ff; his part in breaking relations with Spain, 111 f; at impeachment of Middlesex, 113; and Richard Montague's case, 114 f; controversy with Laud over clerical subsidies, 116 f; and founding of Pembroke College, Oxford, 117 f; present at death of James I, 119; change in his position at accession of Charles, 120 ff; officiates at Coronation, 124; considers Bp Goodman's sermon, 124; refuses to license Sibthorpe's sermon, 127 f; ordered to withdraw to his diocese, 128; suspended from office, 129 f; speeches in 1628 Parliament, 133 f; admonishes Manwaring, 134 f; restored to royal favour, 136; eclipsed by Laud, 136 f; circulates King's instructions to bps, 137; remonstrates with William Page, 138; case of Samuel Pretty, 139, and of William Slater, 139, and of the conventicle at Blackfriars, 139, and of parishioners of St Austin's, London, 140; meeting with Arundel, 141 f; order to parishioners at Crayford, 143 f; last illness, death and funeral, 144; Will, 145 f.
Estimate of his Primacy, 1, 3, 37 ff, 150 ff; his theology, 6 f, 12 ff, 37, 149 f; his preaching, 9 ff, 31; his moral consistency, 70 f, 151;

his personality, 151; his character, 153 f; his hospitality, 40 f, 122; his literary interests, 145 f; his ill health, 78, 81, 87, 89, 91, 108, 124, 127, 141.
Works: *Questiones sex*, 5 f; *Brief Description of the Whole World*, 7 ff; *Exposition on the Prophet Jonah*, 9 ff; *Cheapside Cross Censured*, 19 ff; *Treatise of the Perpetual Visibility ... of the Church*, 21 f; *Reasons which Dr Hill hath brought for upholding of Papistry*, 24 ff; *Examination, Arraignment, and Conviction of George Sprot*, 32.
Abbot, John, 145
Abbot, Maurice (sr), 3 f
Abbot, Maurice (jr), 4, 9, 144
Abbot, Robert, Bp of Salisbury, 4, 65, 71, 84
All Souls College, Oxford, 54, 83, 142 f
Andrewes, Lancelot, Bp of Chichester, Ely, and Winchester, 10, 17, 37, 88, 96, 122, 148; candidate for Primacy, 35 f; relations with Grotius, 49 f, and with Thomas Sutton, 54; Essex divorce case, 58, 59, 62, 64; and Abbot's homicide, 97 ff; absent from James I's deathbed, 119; position at accession of Charles, 120; considers Goodman's sermon, 124
Anne, Queen of England, 50, 78 f, 85 f
Arundel (Thomas Howard), Earl of, 141 f

Bacon, Francis, Lord Verulam, 54, 85, 89
Balliol College, Oxford, 5 f, 20, 117 f
Bancroft, Richard, Bp of London, Abp of Canterbury: estimate of Primacy, 3, 37 f; invites Casaubon to England, 50; controversy over crucifix at Cheapside, 19 f; death, 35; leaves library to Lambeth, 42

INDEX

Essex (Frances Howard), Countess of, ch. 5 *passim*

Frederick V, Elector of the Palatinate, King of Bohemia, 51, 53 f, 87 f, 145

Gerard, John, 23 f
Gloucester, Bp of, *see* Goodman, Godfrey
Goodman, Godfrey, Bp of Gloucester, 124
Gowrie Conspiracy, 31 f
Grindal, Edmund, Abp of Canterbury, 1, 2
Grotius, Hugo, 49 f
Guildford: birthplace of Abbot, 3 ff, 144 f; Hospital of Holy Trinity, 87, 137

Hawkins, Peter, 91 ff, 145
Henry, Prince of Wales (son of James I), 50, 51, 52 ff
High Commission, Court of, 43 ff, 132, 139 f
Hill, Dr Thomas, 24 ff
Huntley (George Gordon), Marquis of, 82 f

James I, King of England: authorizes revision of Bible, 26; relations with Dunbar, 28, 30, 36; visits Oxford University, 29; disapproves of Overall's *Convocation Book,* 29 f; attempts to restore episcopacy in Scotland, 30 f, 33 f; appoints Abbot to Canterbury, 36 f; and Court of High Commission, 45; approves trial and execution of Legate, 46 f; controversy with Vorstius, 47 ff; conversation with Grotius, 50; Spanish match, 51 f, 80, 83 f, 87, 107 ff; influences Essex divorce case, ch. 5 *passim*; relations with Parliament, 74 ff, 88 ff, 105, 110 ff;

and Marquis of Huntley, 82 f; *Declaration of Sports,* 84 f; and the Bohemian Revolt, 87 f; and Abbot's homicide, 93 ff; receives Abp of Spalato, 106; issues "Directions concerning Preachers", 107; death, 119
James, Dr Francis, 59, 69 f
Jegon, John, Bp of Norwich, 47

King, John, Bp of London, 58, 61, 63, 67, 69 f, 76

Lake, Sir Thomas, 36, 50, 53, 67, 70, 77, 106
Laud, William, Bp of St David's, Bath & Wells, Abp of Canterbury, 37, 38, 129, 133, 136, 141, 147, 154; beginning of controversy with Abbot, 21 ff; refuses consecration by Abbot, 94; on Commission to consider Abbot's homicide, 97 ff; consecrated bp, 100; rising influence, 115; and clerical subsidies, 116 f; position and prospects at accession of Charles, 120 f; at Coronation, 123; considers Goodman's sermon, 124; answers Abbot's objections to Sibthorpe's sermon, 126; becomes Bp of London, 135; draws up instructions to bps, 137; on High Commission, 139 f; appointed Abp, 144; estimate of Primacy, 3, 157 f
Legate, Bartholomew, 46 f
Lichfield & Coventry, Bps of, *see* Overall, John; Abbot, George; Neile, Richard
Lincoln, Bps of, *see* Neile, Richard; Williams, John
London, Bps of, *see* Bancroft, Richard; Ravis, Thomas; Abbot, George; King, John; Laud, William
Lubbertius, Sibrandus, 48

172